A Voice in the Wilderness

Mirza Yawar Baig

Table of Contents

Introduction

Some people write poetry. I write prose. Some observe, some reflect, some document, some attempt to create a coherent theory to understand the often chaotic events they witness. I have attempted to do all these all my life. I believe that effective action can only come out of clear understanding about what we experience; both what it means today and what it implies for tomorrow. As they say, 'He also serves who only bears witness.' This book is to bear witness to what has been happening in the world in the past few years. It is the world through my lens. It is not an absolute 'truth'. It is not a ruling or opinion on what should or shouldn't be; though I dare say, some of my own very strong leanings towards social justice, anti-oppression, harmony and peace, do come through.

This book is a witness to what we all lived through and is an attempt to understand it. Hopefully to give you, the reader, an understanding about what the future is likely to be if the same trend continues.

This is a book of hope; my hope that change will be wrought by those who understand the implications of not changing. It is not okay to be comfortable with the social and economic disparities, the injustice and oppression, the double standards and simply the total absence of compassion within ourselves and around us.

This is a world of cause and effect. It has always been because that is the fundamental rule of its creation. What has changed, thanks to technology, is that the time between cause and effect has shortened to make the effect almost instantaneous after the cause. Thanks also to technology, both the cause and effect have become global in influencing minds and hearts. That is very powerful and like all things powerful, potentially very dangerous. Even more important therefore, to ensure that we deal with real causes and not get carried away by the false dreams or demons that we ourselves create using our technology.

The world is still real and will always remain real, no matter how much AI infiltrates it. People will still have hearts and minds, will still love and fear, will still bleed and weep, will still have memories, will still feel hunger, have hopes and aspirations beyond their own lifespans and fears and apprehensions beyond their own existence. To imagine that technology can insulate us from ourselves and our human nature is to display that other tendency—self-deception bordering on insanity, which we have displayed from time to time, to our own detriment and destruction. Some say, 'The only thing we learn from history is that we learn nothing.' Others say, 'Nations that don't learn from history are condemned to repeat it.' I say, 'There is hope as long as we live.' So, this is a book of hope, which records what happened, tries to make sense of it, with the hope that you can take it further to initiating action which can create for us all, a world that is compassionate, caring, prosperous and equitable. Now, what's so bad about that?

Mirza Yawar Baig

Accepting Freedom

I was in South Africa in August 2016, just before the Municipal Elections, a major mood indicator of the nation with respect to the ANC (African National Congress), the party that fought for and got South Africa independence from apartheid. I can't help but recall sadly our (India's) own journey down that road. We achieved independence from foreign rule legally, but have yet to gain independence of the mind. It is for this reason that even today in India, a British national has more status, privileges and aura than an Indian, especially an Indian Muslim or Dalit.

The Indian National Congress which was the party that 'got us independence,' if I may say so, lasted around forty years before it was ousted; its ouster was a result of the same evils of the euphoria of hubris that the ANC seems to be suffering from—the apparent belief that independence was the destination, when it was really the beginning of the journey, even the race. Bringing a nation out of slavery is easy compared to making it own the responsibility of being free. Freedom is in the mind, not in the law books. Free people behave differently because they believe that they're the owners. So they don't steal from themselves, they don't abuse privilege, they don't seek to enrich themselves at the expense of the nation.

That's why in countries like Sweden you have the Prime Minister riding a bicycle to work and nobody finds it extraordinary. It's not a publicity gimmick like our Indian politicians do once in a while. It's normal. Being PM is like being a teacher or a bus driver, all equally dignified and important. Perhaps that's also because Sweden was never a colony, was never subjugated. But countries which have had oppressive governments for generations like South Africa and India have learnt a different equation with the government. India went from monarchy to British colonial rule to democracy. Government was always alien. The few with the power to rule the many. To this day we use the term, Modi's rule, Congress Raj, Collector's Peshi (means 'August Presence'...a Mughal Court term, used today for the District administrator). If you used the term 'rule' for Stefan Löfven they'd laugh you out of town. The titular ruler of Sweden, which is a constitutional monarchy, is King Carl XVI Gustaf who has been King of Sweden since 1973. He is the 74th King of Sweden and also rides a bicycle. He's a ruler akin to the British Queen, more a tourist attraction than a monarch.

Democracy is supposed to be 'government of the people, for the people, by the people'. At least this is what we were taught in school 45 years ago. But for this to happen, it is the people who must be educated and who must understand the meaning of ownership and exercise it. So, whoever may be the political party in parliament, the power always belongs to the people of the nation who give it to a set of leaders to exercise it on their behalf for their (the people's) benefit. Government leaders are analogous to car drivers. The car belongs to the owner. The driver drives it at the pleasure of the owner, as long as the owner employs him, to wherever the owner orders him and then when his day is over, he goes home in his personal transport. That is the actual meaning of government and 'ruling' party in a real democracy. It would never be acceptable for the driver to take the car home or to do with it anything at all without the permission of the owner. The driver will never be the owner of the car no matter how long he drives it. He will always be a driver, judged and rewarded on the basis of his driving and the care he lavishes on the car to keep it in pristine order. But today, whether you look at the drama that's called US elections or in UK or in the many other countries including India and South Africa, you are looking at drivers whose real intentions seem to be to grab the car and dispossess the real owner.

Free nations have dignity. Self-respect is a characteristic of free people which prevents them from being corrupt. You can't steal from yourself but when you see yourself as an outsider you can steal from the "Other". Corruption is a sign that you don't consider yourself to be a part of the nation. Corruption is treason. It is an act of war on the nation. But in some countries, it is rampant, accepted, even aspirational. India and South Africa are not alone in this by any means. This seems to be the fate of almost every erstwhile colony which gained independence after a struggle. All are struggling from the phenomenon of 'Same chairs, different bottoms'. They don't seem to see the fact that it is the chair which must be changed. The change is not in the bottom which sits in the chair, but the mindset which defines what the chair actually means.

The change is by no means easy. It means that people must elect leaders based on principles, ethics, morals and character; not on tribe, caste or community. It means that leaders then have to behave like elected representatives, not like rulers, kings and queens. It means that they must be scrupulously objective, honest, non-partisan and just. It means that integrity, not anything else, must rule every transaction. It means that there must be no financial, social or other benefit in being a leader. It means that we need to take away every 'benefit' that we enjoy today when we are elected to office – yet want to be there only in order to serve.

It means that public servants must reflect, even meditate on the term 'public servant' and consciously accept it as their self-concept. They must act like servants of the public, not as their rulers. It means that we must remove all privilege that goes with so-called public service today in countries like India. It means that almost every reason why most people opt for public service today must be removed. Then only those who still want to serve will be there to serve; quietly, unsung heroes whose love will fill the hearts of those whose difficulty they alleviate. It means we need to create a generation which finds satisfaction from drying people's tears and seeing their smiles.

It means that the public must behave with self-confidence, self-respect and fairness and not demand more than they are due; nor seek privilege over others based on caste, creed, community, tribe or social status. It means that the public must value and want justice, not injustice which they personally benefit from. It means that people must value the law and want to follow it even when it may be painful, because they know that it is good for everyone, including themselves. It means that the law must be superior to people. That crime doesn't pay, criminals do. It means that if a crime is committed, the criminal will be punished no matter who he or she is. No exceptions. That is the meaning of rule of law and what differentiates a democracy from a dictatorship or feudal rule.

It means that the election process itself must be changed where it is the people who pay, not aspiring leaders. As long as elections involve fund raising by candidates, they will breed, even enforce corruption. Good leadership is the need of the people and we the people must pay to have good leaders. It means that campaigning must be dignified with candidates (and parties) speaking about what they have to offer, not spend time in maligning and demeaning others. Elections must not be a circus, nor a drain on the exchequer. Media must be restrained and report facts and give space to information, not become the spokespeople for vested interests and peddle propaganda, innuendo and lies in the name of news. Media must keep itself free from external influence and be the conscience keepers and champions of the values of the nation. It means that accountability must be objective, absolute and unquestioned.

When we are able to accomplish this then and only then, will we be truly free. Only then will we regain our self-respect. Only then will we be able to hold our heads high as a nation that has truly thrown off the chains of servitude. Slavery is in the mind. Subjugated nations become subjugated and remain subjugated because they accept these chains of the superiority of man over man based on external causes; race, position, power, authority or anything else. Equality means to treat yourself as equal to the other – not the other way round. If you say that equality means to treat the other like yourself, you are unconsciously placing yourself at a higher level and feel satisfied at 'bringing' the other to your level. That still means you are doing them a favor. So I prefer to describe it as seeing and treating yourself as equal to the 'other'. In essence, it means eliminating the 'other'. For in a free nation, all people are citizens, albeit with different responsibilities, but all equal to one another and all accountable to the nation which comprises of all of them.

Fantasy, you say? Well, I am a poor old man. Please indulge me. Or accept the fact that when you are far removed from reality, it looks like fantasy. Searching for justice, equity and dignity in our feudal, patriarchal nations, is the real fantasy. Change it or suffer.

Interpreting Reality

Where and how do I begin? To speak from the heart, yet not reveal the grief, confusion and anxiety that it is filled with. Grief at the rapidly deteriorating situation all over the world where human life seems to have lost all value. Confusion as to why this sudden (or is it sudden at all?) collapse of all that I grew up holding valuable and precious? And anxiety, not for myself as much as for the human race in general and for Muslims in particular. I have been troubled by the killing and destruction in recent years, which is rapidly increasing in pace and magnitude. But it was the massacre in the café in Dhaka which forced me to try to write and share my thoughts with those who would like to respond. If you would like to share in the reflection and add your own, I will be most grateful.

The situation globally is as follows:

1. Blatant dichotomy that the Western (read 'White') world applies to itself versus the rest of the world (read 'non-white') where it supports the opposite of the principles it holds sacred and inviolable in its own society. Take freedom, human dignity, human rights, sanctity of human life, child care and protection, justice, equity and compassion – and you will find that Western powers support the opposite in all those places where they have an economic interest. They support, fund and supply the worst dictators to ensure control over their economic interests, turning a blind eye to torture, human rights violations, unlawful imprisonment and

killings, all the while claiming the high moral ground of being 'global policemen' to ensure justice.

The daily reports of Israeli troops using pregnant women for target practice, imprisoning children without reason, and torturing political and war prisoners; proxy wars fought in Muslim lands at the expense of the lives and hopes of the local population; (un)targeted drone strikes legitimizing murder as collateral; Rohingyas being expelled, raped, and slaughtered without pause—the list is endless. Muslims see this as a global conspiracy to annihilate them and wipe Islam off the face of the earth. This leads to a siege mentality and a sense of helplessness and desperation. The thundering silence of Western leaders in this context, especially when compared with their frenzy when a white person is killed by alleged 'Islamic militants', is a study in hypocrisy. As a friend said to me on the deaths of Mohammed Ali and Abdul Sattar Eidhi, *"Whenever a great Muslim dies, he is anything but a Muslim. But whenever a Muslim kills, he is nothing but a Muslim."*

The latest is the revelation (as if it was ever a secret) of the Chilcot Report that the Iraq War was a fabrication of lies led by the Bush-Blair combine, which resulted in the deaths of hundreds of thousands of Muslims, looting of an entire country and destruction of their nation. Question is, what is going to happen to those who are now seen for what they are i.e. murderers and bandits of the worst kind, responsible for genocide of an entire population of innocent people. A rather humorous analysis of it is here:

https://www.theguardian.com/books/2016/jul/10/the-chilcot-report-by-sir-john-chilcot-digested-read-iraq-inquiry

The report itself is on the internet and you are welcome to read it. If some action is taken on this report and Bush and Blair are impeached, then it will restore some trust in global justice. As it is, cynicism far outweighs hope and that is very dangerous. The key question to ask is what every Muslim asks daily, 'What if the situation had been reversed and it was Iraq which had invaded Europe and America?' How would the world have reacted? Are lies alright for white people and not alright for non-white? It is unfortunate to have to keep referencing skin color, but that is the reality of our world.

2. The Muslim world demographically has a very young population which has all the same aspirational goals, attractions and hopes that any average Western youth aspires to, but without the ability to reach them because they are living under prohibitive conditions, thereby condemned to a fate of poverty and deprivation. A young population that is unemployed, poor, has time on its hands, has access to global media, has nothing to lose and feels disenfranchised is dangerous. Alienation born out of poverty and dearth of choices is a reality for the vast majority of Muslim youth in almost every country they live in. Life is a precious gift only for the one who has the means to enjoy it. For those born in

circumstances where life is a burden (materially or psychologically), it is not a gift but something that must be borne willy-nilly. Observably, for some of them (very few perhaps) the moment of perceived glory, of perceived power, where those whom they envied, cringe before them and are at their mercy, is a moment for which they are glad to give up their own lives. They are not afraid to die because to live means nothing to them. They have nothing to lose. They have carried resentment in their hearts against those in society who poured indignity on them; the 'haves' of society and the establishment which they blame for their fate. And so when someone offers them a chance to hit back, they take it. That is what's happening today. People are hitting out blindly, out of frustration, without thinking of the effect of their actions. Disastrous.

3. As another friend, Khadeeja, put it, referring to the attack in the restaurant in Dhaka, *The Dhaka killings were, according to media reports, perpetrated by youth from affluent backgrounds. They went to posh international schools. While economic poverty is a lurking phantom that feeds the cycle of desperation and resulting violence, there is also another kind of poverty among young Muslims, be they from affluent or non-affluent families, which is a poverty of hope that they can change the world. As a result, what we see is an insular way of thinking because of fear/hatred of the Other, of being ridiculed about their idea of Self, even by their own fellow 'secular' Muslims. This kind of insularity*

or perhaps even victim mentality in thought adds fuel to the fire of helplessness. Muslims (and all people with a mind and a conscience) are angry at the rapidly tightening grip of the Military-Industrial Complex (read Western countries) on their lands and resources either directly through military occupation (Palestine, Iraq & Afghanistan) or through proxy rulers (too many to list) and at the blatant disregard for loss of Muslim lives. Culturally, it's become acceptable to disregard or worse, celebrate (films like American Sniper), the killing of Mulsims. The adoption of this inhumanity in the global culture has further served to further their disenfranchisement from the world at large. The extremist statements of people like Trump in America and similar myopic leaders in other countries adds to the anger and the feelings of disenfranchisement.

In the context of this problem definition, the challenge is twofold:

1. Dealing with global aggression, invasion, demonization, blatant injustice and discrimination and the psychological impact it creates
2. Dealing with the helplessness, lack of self-esteem, lack of opportunity and the negative impact of free time and loneliness

So here is my proposal for a solution:

1. Dealing with the effects of global aggression:

I recall going to a Vipasana (Yoga) academy in Bangalore many years ago to learn a relaxation technique called Shavasana. As I was in the class, I overheard a side conversation between the teacher and another student.

Student: I have a problem with acidity. I like to eat chilly and fried things and every time I eat them, I suffer all night with high acidity. Is there a Yoga technique that can help me?

Yoga Teacher: Yes. Stop eating chilly and fried things.

It is really as simple as that. If we, the people of the world, are really tired of dying and losing our lives and livelihoods, then we have to get up and say, 'Enough with this shit.' That means electing leaders who will work to eradicate the war machine, who will take a stand against weapons manufacturers, oil companies, banks, rapacious businesspeople, who will instead commit to alternate energy and environmental protection, spending on education, food and public health. The solution is simple and clear. Some will say it's not practical. But I invite you to reflect on practicality of our current reality: we have given up our freedom and have made ourselves enslaved to immoral political leaders and their handlers – the 1% of the world who run the world. Is it practical to have 1% own 75% of the world's resources and decide the fate of the 99%? Yet, it's our reality. And it is our reality because you and I gave up our control. So, take it back.

We're seeing a sudden surge of dictatorial fascistic leaders around the globe. People give the example of good governance as

Singapore, or Malaysia under Mahatir, or India under Indira Gandhi by saying that the national leader was a CEO. My point is that yes, they were great CEO's and that's precisely what was wrong with them. The fault of the rest of us was that we accepted this arrangement without understanding that what was behind it was a dictatorship; we were happy that the trains ran on time in exchange for our freedoms which were quietly taken away.

Every time anyone protested, the State-Corporation reacted like its business model; put down revolts mercilessly, interpreting dissent as treason and punishing it accordingly. That's why I don't see Arab Sprung (not a typo) and similar movements as winds of change, but as incipient rebellions which will be crushed. The Arab Spring is a case in point. Those who want change will need to do a lot more than marching in the streets. Today, the biggest crime is not what The Empire commits daily, openly and blatantly, but it is to criticize the Empire. The saddest thing is to see this new morality being enforced, not by agents of the Empire, but by hired slave leaders who don't even realize the sad irony—the victims are enforcing their own victimization. How convenient for the oppressors...you get what you want without the bad name that should go with oppression.

Within this global context, the actionable measure for us is to support leaders like Justin Trudeau, Angela Merkel, Jeremy Corbyn, Arvind Kejriwal and others who appear to have kept out of the net of global capitalism. It is equally important to hold them accountable. The Chilcot Report is a good test to see if there's any change in standards in the offing. If there isn't, we must push harder. It is a life and death issue in a very literal sense. Ours and our children's. And we will be held responsible by history.

2. Dealing with alienation and despair

The second problem: Widespread alienation and despair are effects of global injustice. Unless justice is restored, alienation and despair can't be removed. So what I am about to outline is really a symptomatic cure to the systemic cancer that we are plagued with—the greed of those who already own 75% of global assets. I submit to you that this is not a problem of Muslims alone, but a problem that faces 99% of the world. Muslims simply happen to be at the forefront of the receiving end, suffering on behalf of the rest of the world. I submit to you that if the world doesn't come together to establish justice and put an end to the global military-industrial complex and the economics of weapons trade, every single one of us will succumb to this cancer. The model of the 1% enslaving the 99% is not sustainable. Indeed, why should it be?

What is the solution? Give them something to lose.

I believe this has to be done in two ways, simultaneously:

1. Vocational training and entrepreneurial development to boost employment.
2. Ideological dialogue to refute the extremist philosophy that is being projected as Islam.

1. Eradicating Poverty – the most Critical Need of the Hour

A vibrant middle class is essential to the health of any economy and a measure of it. The bigger the middle class, the bigger the market for goods and services. The size of the middle class determines how much money flows into the economy and is available for critical public needs like healthcare, education, transport and so on. Contrary to the myth of trickle down, money doesn't flow down from the superrich or from global multinational corporations into local economies. The superrich don't use local services. They live in ivory tower isolation and are generally unaffected by local conditions, surrounded by cordons of insulation. Multinational corporations are answerable to their shareholders who don't live in local communities and so they don't care what happens in local economies. Many don't even employ local people, except in menial jobs, because locals may not have the education and skills that these jobs need.

So skill development is the key to poverty eradication. For this we need to:

1. Set up vocational training centers in every local school. Every child must mandatorily learn some marketable skill, whether or not he/she uses it later. Working with your hands, working with tools, creating things, fixing broken machinery and such activities are very therapeutic and inspirational. Within technology, we must move

children away from the prevailing sense of consumerism to a service oriented mindset. Most children today know how to download an app, but few know how to make one. Technology, when looked at from a service oriented mindset, has the potential to solve the world's key problems. For example, children can be taught skills in fixing existing technology gadgets than are usable in poor rural areas and can help in generating electricity and providing clean water. There is enough flex in the timetables of our curriculum to permit this and if there isn't then that time must be prioritized. Every child must graduate with a marketable skill. The vocational centers can become self-funded by selling their products and services to local communities and the education can be provided free of cost. That way you will provide employment to local artisans as well as pay for the facility. The infrastructure already exists in the form of the school building. And if necessary, vocational training can also be done after hours when the school has let off.

2. Children must also be taught the basics of entrepreneurship in an easy application oriented way covering the following topics:
    1. Writing a business plan
    2. Budgeting – P&L accounting
    3. Risk taking
    4. Team Building
    5. Selling skills

3. Institute special prizes for entrepreneurial initiatives in key areas like poverty eradication, alternate energy, education, food production, transportation, health management and other high need areas. Prizes must take into account, innovativeness, social consciousness, and creativity.

4. Set up a **Venture Capital Fund** to provide prospective entrepreneurs with interest free loans. These must be given after a rigorous selection process of examining business plans and ensuring that they have a high likelihood of success. The capital for this fund can come from partnering corporations as part of their Corporate Social Responsibility (CSR). I know this is being done by some progressive CEO's but it must be hugely boosted. CEO's will recognize the value of such a fund and will fully support it. Invite them to sit on the Board and run it.

5. Pair new entrepreneurs with established businessmen and women who can coach and mentor them. This will break the economic/social barriers, which have taken the place of feudal barriers of old, but have the same negative effects. Wealthy people must see how the poor live. It touches the heart. It makes us human and above all, grateful for what we have and the desire to share it with others.

2. Ideological support

It is a given today that there are people on the internet, who are spreading hatred and recommending all kinds of violence in the name of Islam. It is a redundant discussion in my mind about whether these are false flag operations or genuinely misguided Muslims who are spreading this message. The fact remains that they are spreading it and there are some Muslim youth who are attracted enough to it to wreak havoc.

What happened in Dhaka was not done by an army. It was done by a few people and rocked the world. That is the aim of the anarchist—hit soft targets that are impossible to defend and create disruption in society to further their own aims. Society's reaction, be it police brutality, media hysteria or racist and fascist statements by politicians, are all further blessings for the recruiter as they only help to reinforce the anti-establishment message and enhance the feeling of persecution that the potential recruits feel. The situation therefore needs extreme maturity, patience, fortitude and wisdom to handle. Like the economic strategy, this must also be seen as a long term investment. Changing hearts is a notoriously difficult thing to do. Ideological conflicts are the worst and most difficult to resolve, but resolve we must. Our lives, quite literally depend on it. I suggest the following steps:

Restore confidence in Government and in the Justice System

I won't go into the reasons why this is perhaps at an all-time low. I want to focus on what we can do to change that situation. We can't influence people who don't trust us and so trust must be built. We must decriminalize legitimate dissent.

Else, we risk having the bottled-up anger and frustration unleashed through violent reactions. When governments suppress legitimate forms of political dissent, often violently, they risk radicalization and people resorting to violence for their voices to be heard. We have seen many examples of this all over the Middle East in the recent past.

Establish Justice

All criminals must be punished, but only criminals must be punished.

It is as simple as that. Give people a door to legal redressal and they will not take the law into their own hands. Help criminals believe that they can't get away with their crimes because of their caste, tribe or political affiliation. That is the meaning of justice. One law for everyone irrespective of who he or she is. This will restore confidence and go a very long way to wean people away from extremist ideology. Take away the reason for resentment. Take away their desperation. Take away their hopelessness and despair. Or be prepared for them to burst into flames, consuming all those around them.

It is essential that governments don't officially support those (especially Muslims) who criticize Islam, mock the Prophet ﷺ or mock religious scholars. If this is not done, then anything run by the government will be rejected. Suspicion is a hurdle that will have to be surmounted in any case for any government funded program and can only be done by winning the confidence of scholars that people trust. That can only be done if there is genuine respect. Acting cannot be sustained and trust lost can never be regained. People are entitled to their opinions and if someone wants to criticize Islam they are welcome to do so but governments must be neutral. That way people don't feel persecuted. Equality means equal protection.

This is our choice. Our time is running out. We must act. We must act in concert because this concerns us all. We are all in it together.

Enforce transparency across all law enforcement

Transparency is essential. Follow due process with transparency and treat people with dignity. I won't describe what happens today when someone (especially a Muslim) is arrested on suspicion and his family go to the police station to enquire. I know that those who will read this are fully aware of what happens. The problem is what this has done to the image of the police in particular and of the justice system in general. People have lost hope in both. Radicalization starts with this and is fed by every incident where justice is perverted and denied by those who have authority. Transparency is essential. Justice must be seen to be done.

I propose that when someone is to be arrested on suspicion, there must be enough incriminating evidence before the arrest warrant is issued. Then this evidence must be shown to the family of the individual and his lawyers and credible members of his community so that it becomes clear to everyone that there is indeed sufficient ground for the arrest. Our current reality, it must be recognized, is that thanks to social stigma and irresponsible reporting, a person who is arrested is already tried and condemned before he reaches a court of law. So even when he is found to be innocent, his life is effectively destroyed. He loses his job, he and his family face a social boycott and sometimes have to move to a different town. All this not because he was guilty at all, but because the police made a mistake. Having others suffer because of your mistakes is not justice, is it? Transparency is key to restoring confidence. Involving the public through good communication is essential to good policing, especially in fighting terrorist activity.

Believe me, we the people are even more interested in fighting terrorist activity for the simple reason that we die when it happens. So involve people and don't treat them like potential criminals. Muslims know what is happening in their community far better than any policeman can ever know and will gladly help in preventing and solving crime if they are taken into confidence, are trusted and treated with dignity. This is sadly missing in police public interaction at a grassroots level. Our police have become used to behaving in a highhanded, arrogant manner because they can get away with it. People suffer in silence because they have no alternative. But trust is destroyed, which is our current situation. This must be built with great patience and wisdom.

Police – Public Communication & Sensitization

The police have become used to being the coercive arm of government. The primary role of the police officer should be as a partner of the public in keeping them safe. The two roles can't coexist. So we need to choose. If police public partnership works, coercion will become unnecessary except in exceptional circumstances which will be understood by all concerned. Communication is key for this to happen.

As a test of my claim that police officers maintain an intimidating distance from the people, which discourages participation, here is a checklist that you can give to the Station House Officer (SHO) of any Police Station to fill out. The results will be enlightening, and I hope they will encourage the seniors to action by presenting an example of this behavior. Juniors usually imitate seniors and we have plenty of examples to show of pompous seniors who won't even answer a phone, let alone talk politely to a civilian. So send this checklist to all SHO's and see what they say:

1. How many prominent local people do you know personally?
2. How many of them are without political affiliation and from minorities or Dalits?
3. How many of them do you visit socially at least once a year?
4. Do you invite them to any function at the PS - e.g. Independence Day flag hoisting?
5. If not, why not?

6. Do you participate, even if by simply wishing, in any festival not your own?

7. If not, why not?

8. Do you visit any schools, hospitals, NGO's, places of worship in your area?

9. If not, why not?

You can add any more questions as you wish but I believe the results will be the same. Police don't have a relationship with the public because they don't want to. If Indian Police really want to be partners with the public, then they have to define who they are and what their role is. You can't run with the hare and hunt with the hounds. You have to decide where you belong and act accordingly.

Sensitivity Training for the Police

One of the first courses I taught at the SVP National Police Academy was for IPS Probationers of the 1991 batch on Police Public Sensitization. This was a course mandated at the time by the Home Ministry and I believe it was one of the best initiatives of government which must be reinstated. A nation can't progress when it lives in a state of war with its own people. There are over 200 million Muslims in India who are all good, law abiding and peaceful citizens, who love their country and are committed to its well-being to which their own well-being is attached. Sadly, they have been put into the insulting position of having to declare their loyalty over and over again only to be disbelieved. Especially in officialdom, the police usually being its first encounter, they are viewed with suspicion – guilty until proven innocent – regardless of the lack of evidence against them. Committing crimes is not the copyright of any community. Crime must be treated as crime, not as proof of collective evil of any community. Fairness is the foundation of justice. It is therefore essential to educate the police about Islam's fundamental beliefs and tenets so that they are not susceptible to propaganda that Islam is somehow the cause of violence. They must also be trained in behaving with sensitivity and in treating the civilian population as partners in solving crime. Bridges must be built and policemen and women need to be trained in how to do this. If anyone is in doubt about this, let him go incognito to a police station disguised as an ordinary Muslim father of a son arrested on suspicion and experience the fun. The dignity of the individual must always be respected.

The law can't be upheld by those who break the law. Police must uphold the law in letter and spirit and the use of torture and so-called 3rd degree methods must be outlawed and their perpetrators punished. It is good to remember that our legal system doesn't permit these reprehensible methods in any case. But the police have become so accustomed to using them that it may sound strange to some to remind them that their actions as policemen are illegal.

Finally, we must hold the media accountable for the harm they create. 'Trial by media' has become a standard practice where character assassination is a rite of passage for any citizen embroiled in a controversy. Anchors and writers hide behind terms like 'alleged,' 'reported' and 'believed' and proceed to hold their own trial before even an ounce of evidence is discussed in the court of law. This loss of consciousness, driven by the greed to achieve higher TRP ratings, by the people who are responsible for bringing us unbiased information is irresponsible, despicable and shameless. To combat the widespread spin and misinformation coming out of mainstream media, we must do more to establish an independent network of factcheckers who can separate the fact from fiction for people and just as importantly, provide a real-time honesty percentage for the news networks. This would help create a much-needed oversight for the news organizations and also help viewers make better decisions around where they go for their information.

It is high time that journalists realize their respected purpose so that they understand the need to regain it. The media is the last defence of the innocent civilian. If the media persecutes that person for the sake of cheap popularity, then it is a case of Jab manjhi nayya duboye usay kaun bachaye?

Imam Development Program

The influence of the local Imam is huge. He is seen as a confidant who has knowledge of Islam and so is often listened to with great attention. Sadly, many, if not most, Imams are not trained to lead. Their knowledge is restricted to a very small section of Islam and the Imam does not have the perspective or tools to interpret current events or to guide his congregation. He can't admit that openly as he needs to maintain his aura of being knowledgeable to retain his job.

The challenge is to handle this with great empathy, sensitivity and understanding, working with mainstream scholars who the Muslim community trusts. You have to first win over these scholars and then make them the ambassadors for this program. There is a huge suspicion among Muslims for anything that seems to come from government, police, foreign agencies, born out of their own bitter experience in the past. Winning them over will not be easy, but extremely necessary. Scholars will be very wary of associating with any program that an NGO runs for fear of losing their own credibility with their constituencies. To try to force them would be suicidal. What we need is a lot of patience, perseverance and genuine sincerity which I am sure will help them to see the value of the Imam Development Program.

I suggest using the Minorities Commission or a respected NGO as the front for this program as they have better credibility and to do it without fanfare and flashbulbs. It is necessary to handle this with great care because if it loses credibility with the community then the cycle of distrust will deepen and prevent progress.

Imam Development Program must be funded and should be

free for students (Imams), held over a duration of 3 – 6 months as a part-time course covering the following areas:

1.   Understanding current events (no propaganda – just honest appraisal)

2.   How to make the masjid a window into the Muslim life & culture

3.   Cross cultural sensitivity, interfaith dialogue, community service

4.   Refuting the message of the extremist from the Islamic ideological angle

5.   Answering questions about current challenges in an Islamic context

6.   Counseling skills

7.   Public speaking skills

Finally, we have to answer the question for the potential student – the Imam who we hope will come to this program – WiiFM? What's in it for me? The reason I say this is because in India at least (my guess is this will be the same more or less, elsewhere), Imams are paid very poorly by the masjid where they serve. Most congregations have little money and so they pay the Imam what they can and he makes up the balance by giving private tuitions, teaching children to read the Qur'an for 45-60 minutes per class, going house to house. Imams lead an extremely busy lifestyle. In addition to these private tuitions, they must also be present in the mosque for the five prayers. Therefore, the Imam Development Program must be scheduled around their schedule and be easily accessible. Additionally, the program must offer a stipend as a financial incentive for the Imams to join despite their busy lifestyle. A certificate from the government, Department of Education or some such department could also serve as an added attraction.

Where are we headed?

You may have seen the famous documentary, Four Horsemen.

https://www.youtube.com/watch?v=5fbvquHSPJU

In this film is this quote:

When plunder becomes a way of life for a group of people living together in society, they create for themselves in the course of time, a legal system that authorizes it and a moral code that glorifies it.   ~ Frederic Bastiat

I ask myself why it is that we have written history to eulogize and applaud every rapacious bandit? Why is Alexander of Macedonia called, "The Great"? And a host of other bandits from every part of the world, whose only contribution was mass destruction, enslavement of innocent people and looting the resources of their countries. The British, Spanish, Portuguese, French, Dutch and German Empires did their best to outdo each other in this race. Now the Americans are trying to beat the rest. I can't be bothered to name all the others who I have missed not because of forgetfulness but out of contempt for this whole line of thinking and living.

As long as we continue to glorify war and plunder, we will continue to be plundered. That is the paradigm and conversation that we must change.

I am not for getting too stuck in our own theories and start treating them like fundamental laws. They are not. They are theories; our attempts to make sense of our world. All power to those who postulate them and reflect on them. But they are theories. The world, the earth, is not something we understand completely – to put it mildly – for I believe we don't understand it at all. Comparing the human race to rats or bacteria in a petri dish only goes so far. These are not absolute conclusions to be applied to ourselves.

In any case, even if they were absolute, we have two choices: Lie down and die, or work like hell to change the conclusions. I opt for the latter. I would rather go out on my feet fighting for a better world.

That is why I say to myself, **'I will not allow what is not in my control to prevent me from doing what is in my control.'**

Controlling world population is not in my control. But to reduce my own carbon footprint, to share my resources, to help others and many other things are very much in my control. So, I try to do all these.

As for the articles on population control, I have read similar themes in them for at least over 30 years. They predicted the end of the earth at lower population levels (less than 8 billion). But we are still here. The general perspective propagated by these articles is to reduce the population in some remote land where the people are foreign. This concept of 'other' makes it easier to conceptualize these populations as culls. Easy because they are not like 'Us". Shades of smallpox infected blankets to Native Americans?

We enable ourselves into this highly homicidal way of thinking because we think within the artificial and false boundaries of our nation states; lines on maps of our own making. We forget that the earth is not like this. Africa is not different from America or Asia because we decide to draw a line or because there is a ditch which we call the Atlantic between it and America. The earth is connected. It is ONE. Whether we like to accept that or not. What happens to one will happen to all of us, whether we like it or not. Ref: Butterfly effect.

The only way therefore that we can 'save ourselves' is by saving others. Not by culling them. Call it what you want but that is the conclusion that all these theories of 'population control' are leading to. It is this thinking – I don't need to change, but the population needs to be reduced – that produces our Eternal War philosophy. Military Industrial States need war to survive and grow. They need to build weapons, places to use them with impunity and guess what, the reward is two separate lines of revenue; weapons sales and picking up the pieces later in the form of mines, oil, loot, slaves and land.

Who does all that go to? The 1% (62 people). Those same 62. At whose cost? All the poor dumb morons who thought they were fighting for honour, to save their glorious lands from the marauding hordes of barbarians who don't know the taste of a Big Mac or Pepsi. Okay, Coke. Same difference. It takes two to tango. In this case, the spin doctors who write the script to suit the 1% and the dumb, unwashed multitude who believes this complete crap and are willing to lay down their lives so that the 62 are not deprived of a single fish egg of their caviar. As long as there are those who are willing to be exploited, the exploiters will have a field day. That is why I say that it is high time we – the 99% - wake up. At least die with your eyes wide open.

I am of the belief that we need to change our lifestyles, which will stem from changing our values and rejecting the capitalistic, global domination model that we have been raised to believe. We must reject, greed and demonstrate that by ending our endless collection of garbage in the name of shopping, our addiction to self-aggrandisement and appeasing desires, our enslavement to accumulation of personal wealth at all cost and our world view which places us at the centre with everyone and everything else subordinate and subservient to ourselves. All of this is eminently possible with the right education starting in primary schools.

After all, if someone had told us to create a system where 62 people would have more wealth than the bottom 50% of global population, we would have laughed them out of the room. But that is exactly what we have accomplished and that too so subtly and quietly that I bet not one of us even realised it was happening. But believe me, we did it. We legitimized lying with full eye contact (recall George Bush and Colin Powell and Iraq's unfindable Weapons of Mass Destruction), legitimized treating others like flies or mosquitos, to be exterminated (recall Madelaine Albright's comment on ABC: that the deaths of half a million Iraqi children was 'worth it': https://www.youtube.com/watch?v=omnskeu-puE) and legitimized hypocrisy at levels perhaps never before seen. Come on people, wake up! Everything has an effect.

I say that because if we did this, we can undo it. We must undo it. It can't last. It is a criminal, grossly unjust and utterly criminal way of life.

The earth will correct itself. It will get rid of the cancer that is polluting it. It has seen many cycles of catastrophic (for its inhabitants, not for the earth itself) changes that completely altered the composition of those who live on it. And it can and will do it again.

So, let us get ready to change. Or get ready to be changed.

In Search of Peace – Really?

What is required for peace to prevail?

Anything done with a clear intention and according to a system gives value added results.

Take the case of calisthenics – weight lifting – to build strength. And compare it to the most common cause of a strained back and lower back injury – weight lifting. How is it possible that the same thing is beneficial and harmful at the same time?

The answer lies in the method. In the first instance, you follow a system and do the actions deliberately with a clear intention under the guidance of an expert, at least initially. In the latter, you just grab a weight and lift it – most commonly a heavy piece of luggage at a railway or airport, lacking a system and conscious intention.

In his book 'Talent is Overrated', Geoff Colvin talks about 'deliberate practice' as distinct from 'distracted practice' – distracted is my term – but what he means is that simply hitting a thousand golf balls a day will do nothing to improve your swing or take away your slice if it is not done deliberately, consciously and under expert guidance – meaning according to a system. In the latter case hitting far fewer balls will do more for your swing that hitting a thousand a day.

So how does this apply to peace? If we are serious about peace we need to answer two questions:

1. Do we really want peace?
2. Are we willing to do what it takes to achieve peace?

Let us look at some data because as they say, 'Data doesn't lie.' Here is a graph showing the return on investment of armament manufacturers.

Company	Lobbying	Federal Contracts
Boeing Co	$15.9 million	$22.1 billion
Lockheed Martin	$15.1 million	$41.5 billion
United Technologies	$14.2 million	$8 billion
Northrop Grumman	$12.8 million	$14.4 billion
General Dynamics	$11.4 million	$19.7 billion

Between 2001-2011 the defense industry as a whole spent $1.2billion on lobbying and on average employed nearly 1,000 lobbyists annually – nearly two for every member of

Congress. It contributed \$24.4 million to political candidates in the 2011/2012 election cycle alone. A ROI of \$22.1 billion on an expense of \$15.9 million (Boeing) is astronomical. Impossilbe figured for any field other than gambling perhaps. But in this industry it is not a gamble.

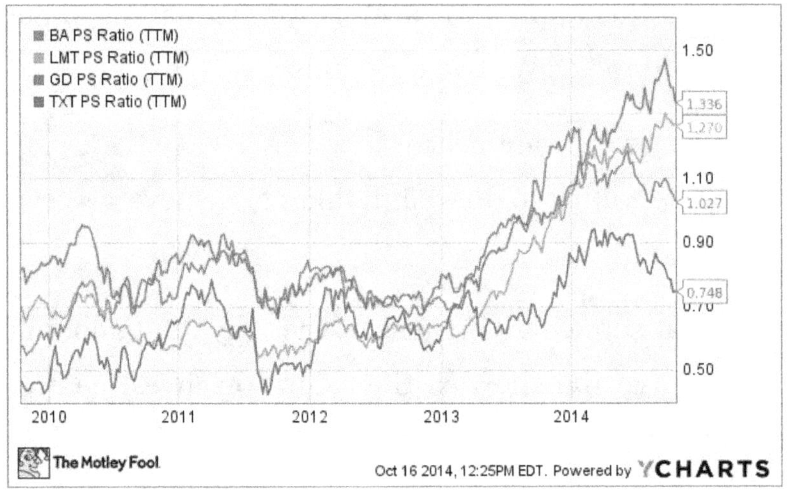

Here is what the top four defence stocks did since the Iraq war. So that explains the imagination of the creators of WMD's and the proponents of that theory who felt no shame in lying through their teeth before the UN. That's why I fall off my chair laughing when anyone tries to peddle 'Leadership Lessons' of Gen. Colin Powell.

Let us look at who makes all this happen

Table 2. The 10 largest importers of major weapons and their main suppliers, 2010–14

Importer	Share of international arms imports (%)		Main suppliers (share of importer's total imports), 2010–14		
	2010–14	2005–2009	1st	2nd	3rd
India	15	7	Russia (70%)	USA (12%)	Israel (7%)
Saudi Arabia	5	1	UK (36%)	USA (35%)	France (6%)
China	5	9	Russia (61%)	France (16%)	Ukraine (13%)
UAE	4	5	USA (58%)	France (9%)	Russia (9%)
Pakistan	4	3	China (51%)	USA (30%)	Sweden (5%)
Australia	4	3	USA (68%)	Spain (19%)	France (6%)
Turkey	3	3	USA (58%)	South Korea (13%)	Spain (8%)
USA	3	3	Germany (18%)	UK (15%)	Canada (13%)
South Korea	3	6	USA (89%)	Germany (5%)	Sweden (2%)
Singapore	3	3	USA (71%)	Germany (10%)	Sweden (6%)

And then take the case of one of these importers and see the situation at home

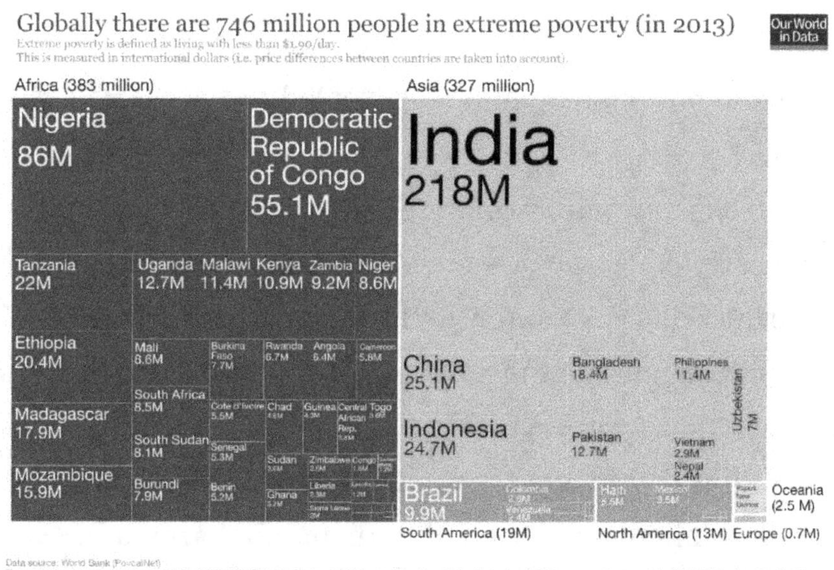

Why would a country with the greatest abject poverty and in no real danger from anyone want to spend a fortune importing arms? You tell me.

And finally to prove how beneficial wars are for those who run them here's more data:

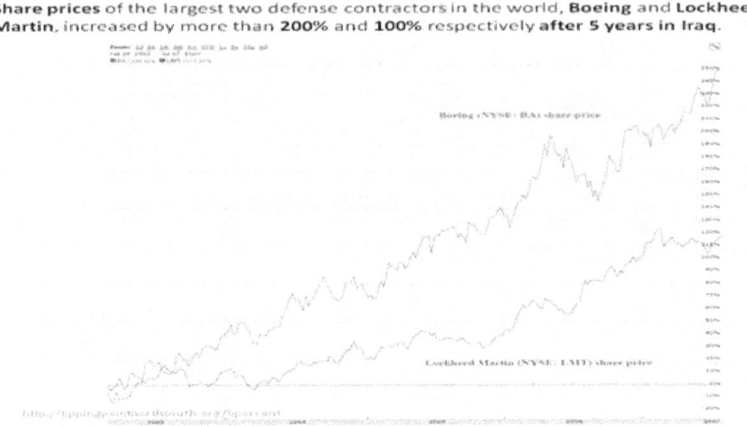

Consider our popular culture in the light of these facts and you will see why we glorify war and soldiers both in history as well as at present. Armies sell the story that they exist to protect civilians who owe them a debt of honor. That is true for armies that exist purely for defence and don't invade and occupy and pillage others. But what about the great armies of the nations who have historically colonised other nations and to this day are engaged in wars of oppression, invading and looting nations who did them no harm and who represented no threat? Are these defending their people or serving their commercial masters? How honorable is such soldiering?

Ask yourself some questions:

1. We have all read about Alexander, The Great. We were taught in school always to use the title 'The Great' when referring to Alexander. What makes him great? He invaded lands, destroyed homes, killed people, enslaved the free, raped and plundered and became rich on the spoils of war. That makes him 'The Great'?

2. What about those who resisted him, fought to defend their homes and families? Who was more honorable? The invader or the defender? The bandit or the householder who fights the bandits to save his family?

3. Check out the meaning of 'spoil'. Then ask why even war mongers call them 'spoils of war'?

4. The word 'Caesar' has entered the language itself to mean King. Ask why, when Julius Caesar, the first Consul of Rome to hold that title, was not a king at all and on slaughtering one million Gauls remarked, 'Today was a good day.'

5. Ask this question about all conquerors of all times. No exceptions.

6. Ask why we have always glorified conquerors and cast resistance fighters in the role of villians, calling them 'insurgents', 'rebels', 'terrorists' etc?

7. Ask why we call killing innocent civilians, 'collateral damage'? Put your children in the place of the dead ones and then say 'collateral damage'.

8. Ask how else can you demonstrate the effectiveness of weapons unless you create a situation where you legalize their use, glorify murderers and demonize defenders?

According to one African maxim, "Until Lions write their own history, the tale of the hunt will always glorify the hunter." - See more at: http://www.elginism.com/similar-cases/until-lions-write-their-own-history-the-tale-of-the-hunt-will-always-glorify-the-hunter/20080410/1088/#comment-92559

Looting in the name of civilizing nations that British and other colonials did is an old story and it continue today. One day someone will have to catalogue and write about the Iraqi artefacts that were stolen after 'liberation' of Iraq, both from Saddam and its art and treasure. Truly Iraqis must feel so free now. Don't even ask about the Kohinoor diamond in the British Crown and where that came from and a million other things that were looted from India, Africa and Asia. When theft is glorified in the name of conquest, then there is no shame in wearing the proceeds of it in the crown.

But you say you want peace?

War is profitable. Hugely profitable. There will be war as long as there is profit in it. Want peace? Make war unprofitable. Quod Erat Demonstrandum.

What Happened – 2014 Indian Parliamentary Elections

If there is one word that best describes the results of the 2014 Indian Parliamentary Elections, it is SURPRISE. For some it was a very pleasant surprise – for others it was a nasty shock. But nobody including the paid analysts had really any clue how close they were to the truth when they were predicting a landslide victory to the BJP.

Today in 1947, we gained freedom from the British...

But who'll free us from corruption,
poverty, immorality and greed?

We Enslave Ourselves.

So first some congratulations are in order:

Congratulations to the BJP for running a brilliant campaign and being able to influence the mind of the voter. Narendra Modi was decisive, communicated incessantly, used the media with aplomb, took every advantage that came his way including the six week staggered voting mechanism, capitalized on a cadre of dedicated people who did him proud and stuck exclusively to a development agenda which resonated with the common man. The fact that the BJP was voted out of power after Gujarat 2002 was not ignored. This time around, the BJP stayed clear of the RSS inspired Hindutva agenda and leveraged the good governance in the States where they had the government to promise the same in the country. The hard work and complete dedication of the RSS/BJP cadre can only be admired and applauded. Modi didn't exaggerate when he said that it was because of them that he won the election. That is a fact they can be proud of.

Congratulations to this great nation of ours for being able to run an election of this magnitude in a fair and orderly manner and then compiling results which today are so clearly accepted as being fair and accurate that nobody even thinks of challenging them or claiming that the election was rigged. Hats off to the Election Commission for a sterling job that we as Indians can truly be proud of and boast about.

Congratulations also to the Congress for being so spectacularly blind to the writing on the wall, even though it was in the form of an electronic, neon lit bill board in pulsating psychedelic lights, predicting its demise. An epitaph must necessarily be brief.

Congratulations to the Muslims for being divided so fragmentally that for the first time in our post-independence history the famous 'Muslim vote' that everyone respected and feared was rendered completely ineffective. UP with all the major Madaaris and Aligarh Muslim University and some districts with over 40% Muslim voters didn't get Congress a single seat in Parliament. If that doesn't show that Muslims voted for the BJP then what else does it show?

So how did this happen?

1. **Hubris:** Congress was living in a world of make-believe living off a legacy that had really dried up at least a decade earlier but even the final wet mud at the bottom of the pool went dry now. Failure of dynasty politics – one hopes it has truly failed and will not merely be replaced by another dynasty – in a nation that is more used to kings and dynasties

than to democracy is something to be pleased about in itself. Next step, hopefully, will be leadership based on ethical and moral principles and not on caste – but maybe I am stretching it.

2. **BJP:** Ran a campaign completely devoid of the Hindutva agenda of its previous incarnation. It spoke of good governance, justice, economic empowerment and inclusiveness. So one must ask if this is what got them the votes – and not the RSS inspired Hindutva mandir/anti-Muslim agenda. After all the fact that the BJP won 73 out of 80 seats in UP shows that Muslims voted for them – which in itself was totally unexpected – until one considers the spectacular failure of Mulayam Singh's Samajwadi Party, elephantine megalomania of Mayawati's BSP and the sleepwalking of Congress. Then what was unexpected becomes logical.

We can only forget or ignore the power of culture and history at our own peril. We are a nation that has a 5000 year history of kings and just 65 years of democracy. In that 5000 year history, we never rebelled against a king. We worship strength and power. We see kindness and compassion as weakness. Greatness is defined in our culture as the ability to break the law with impunity. This 'greatness' extends to a 'great man's' servants and followers and so to be associated with a 'great man' is seen as a personal advantage. A 'great man' in our culture is one who can protect those who do his bidding regardless of right or wrong. Modi projected himself as that 'great man' – the electorate proved that he was accepted in this role.

Today, we consider corruption merely as cost of doing business to be factored into our rates and costs and justified by the benefits that accrue. Corruption is now in our blood and has changed from being an aberration to an aspiration. There is no stigma attached to it at any level. It is merely seen as payment for service. It is only when we pay and don't get the service that we complain – which is what happened in the Congress government. Equality, egalitarianism, social causes, ideology and even justice is seen by most Indians as interesting at best – but not something we are willing to invest in or will commit to live by. The demise of the Trade Unions and the Communist Party and the decimation of the BSP (Dalit Party) in UP are cases in point. We are a selfish people – we look for personal benefit above all else. Modi promised us personal benefit and we believed him. It remains to be seen what he is able to deliver – but the Sensex reflects this public optimism.

3. **Divisions:** 2014 was a year characterized by one spectacular meteor flying across the political horizon - clad in a funny cap and a muffler round his neck, broom in hand – Arvind Kejriwal – who like a meteor seems to have crashed in flames. However, while he was in flight, he emanated the light of hope – the hope of clean government, power to the common man, nemesis of the big business-brigands who populate our corridors of power and an end to our crippling corruption. He upset everyone's calculations in Delhi elections; he trounced Congress and rendered Sheila Dixit homeless and then didn't occupy the house to which he was entitled, thereby presenting Manmohan Singh with his own retirement home. Many voted for him or really for what he stood for. But not enough to save him or his own seat. Imagination not converted into a ballot box victory. Good case in point about the power of decisiveness and the failure of philosophy. We are very pragmatic people who like definite things. Arvind Kejriwal miscalculated and didn't realize that philosophy doesn't sell. Neither does being slapped in public – it may get you pity – but it doesn't get you respect. Calling it 'Gandhian' is incorrect because Gandhiji was never slapped by any Indian and in any case he never had to win any election. We Indians want a powerful decisive leader – not one who can't even protect himself from being slapped.

Costly miscalculation for Kejriwal. Sad for all who supported him.

Using UP as a good example of what happened across the country – on one side was the committed BJP voter who would come out in 48°C temperatures to cast his vote for his party. On the other side was the Congress/Secular party voter who had to choose between BSP, Samajwadi, AAP, Congress and many smaller parties – and he did – all to the benefit of the BJP. So in a manner of speaking the BJP is beholden to all those who voted for Congress, BSP, Samajwadi, AAP and others for its spectacular victory.

It shows also that the single minded interest of the voter is an economic agenda in pursuit of which he is able to forgive and forget everything else. No matter how unsavory and unidealistic this sounds, this appears to be the reality of the Indian voter across all divides. Another contributing factor is the quality of the Muslim leader – Mukhtar Ansari is a case in point – who is so completely pathetic and uninspiring that it is little wonder that they chose Modi over him. So would you and I. The Ulama, engrossed as they have been in their internal conflicts for the past several years, completely unconnected with their constituents, were rendered completely ineffective, including those who entered politics – after all if you join the party of (Mukhtar Ansari), a convicted criminal, what else do you expect than to be ignored – and good riddance. Walking the talk is essential. If you talk unity and walk dispute it costs. Wonder if our Ulama will learn the lesson.

Now that this has happened and we all seem to be in a state of shock – the big question is what must we Muslims do? In my view, we need to do the following which will be difficult and bitter but then the alternative is even more bitter to contemplate. I hope we are able to see the reality of what we face and have the guts to do what we need to do if we really want to ensure a secure future for generations yet unborn. Do we have it in us to act? History will bear witness.

Winners are not those who don't fall. Winners are those who get up the quickest. Not just get up – because everyone eventually gets up – but get up fast.

1. The first and foremost thing to do is to remind ourselves and others that we Muslims are the citizens of India – with one cardinal difference – our fathers chose to live here when they had the option to go to Pakistan. Others who live here had no option. We did and we chose to live in India. India is

our country. We don't need anyone's permission to live here and neither do we need to prove our loyalty to anyone. India is our country – we live in it and for it and we will die in it and for it. Patriotism is loyalty to our nation, not loyalty to any political party. We are patriotic and nobody has the right to question our patriotism and we don't have to defend it or to answer anyone who is ignorant enough to question it. This is our land, the Constitution of which guarantees us the same rights as every other citizen, irrespective of caste, creed or religion. This is our land in which we are equal to every other citizen of every other caste, creed or religion. We stand for India and against anyone who is an enemy of our country. This is my land – our land – the land of our forefathers and the land of our generations unborn, yet to come. It is from this mindset that we must proceed.

2. We have lived in this land from times immemorial. Muslims have been in India for the past 1389 years, beginning from 625 AD (4 Hijri) when the first Arabs came to Kerala and locals accepted Islam. What ancient Muslim rulers did during their rule – both the good and bad - is not our responsibility; we weren't alive then. Neither is what happens or

doesn't happen in Pakistan, Saudi Arabia or any other so-called Muslim country.

3. What is relevant is our own history where we the Muslim people were at the forefront of the Independence movement where our leaders fought alongside their compatriots and were imprisoned and killed by the British Colonial power.

4. In modern India, our Madrassa system educates more than 2 million children free of cost, which costs the community Rs.12 billion per annum. There is no other community in India who spends this kind of money on educating its people, which is really the responsibility of the Government of India as we are Indian citizens.

We are Indians and India is our concern. This is our reality and it does not change whoever comes to power.

For anyone who is interested in the welfare of this nation I must say that Indian Muslims are 20% of the population – it can be a force to reckon with in respect to buying power, economic drive and stability, if it is harnessed by investment in its development, or a drag threatening to drown the nation if it is discriminated against, oppressed and driven to the wall. I don't see anyone with any intelligence wanting to make enemies of 200 million of its own citizens. That would be suicidal.

There are two possible scenarios that the BJP victory predicts:

1. That the BJP lives by its stated agenda of good governance, economic development and eradicating corruption. In that case this portends good for the Muslims who can look forward to development programs and real upliftment from poverty and deprivation. For the nation it can only mean great benefit because economically empowering 200 million people is to empower the whole nation. We need to give the BJP the benefit of the doubt and take them at their word and wait to see if they live up to it. Logically they should because they are certainly intelligent people. The future will tell.

2. The BJP brings out its earlier RSS inspired agenda of oppressing Muslims and using them as a scapegoat and allows our brigand-businesses to have the field and make hay and more while the

saffron sun shines. I don't think I need to describe that scenario. Its results can only be imagined. The reality will be worse. In that case what will be, will be. Living in terror expecting the worst makes no sense. Living with hope, does.

Irrespective of what future unfolds, it is up to us to decide what we must do.

So what must we Indian Muslims do? Here's what I believe we must do.

 Be resilient. Get up from the floor. Accept reality and take stock. The thing that distinguishes nations that endure is not bravery or strength but resilience. The ability to simply stay in the race, no matter how many or how bad the knocks.

There are three steps to resilience:
    a. Face the brutal facts but don't lose hope
    b. Make sense of what is happening
    c. Take hard decisions to ensure the future

Face the Brutal Facts: So what are the brutal facts with respect to the political history of Muslims in post-independence India?

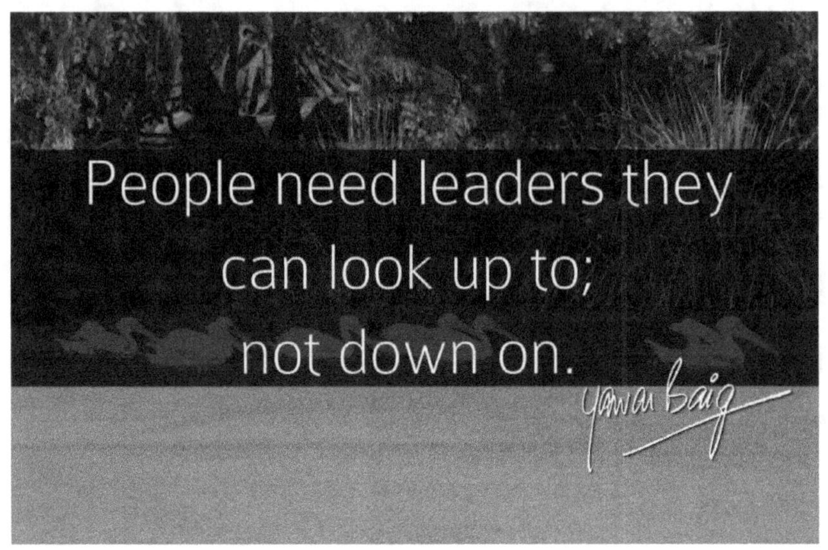

In one word – deteriorating quality of leadership. We have been on a slide and the end is not in sight yet. No vision, strategy, unity or discipline. Just bravado, loud mouthed speeches. Our leaders are true to type with the kind of mercenary, corrupt leadership that we have been plagued with in India. Our leaders are as corrupt and mercenary as anyone else with absolutely nothing to distinguish them as Muslims. Islam is not a differentiator except as a convenient tool for them to whip up emotions to serve their own short sighted political agendas. Our leaders are politicians in the worst sense of the term and not the statesmen that we need.

Congress, in one form or another, ruled this country since independence except for one term when the BJP (NDA) occupied the throne in Delhi. In that long period of over 5 decades, every atrocity that was done to Muslims, from the demolishing of the Babari Masjid, to the so-called Bombay pogrom, Bhagalpur pogrom, Makkah Masjid blasts, the latest pogrom in Muzzafernagar and a million others, as well as the gross neglect of and discrimination against Muslims, all happened under Congress rule at the Center. The BJP not to be left behind allowed the Gujarat pogrom to take place during their watch. Then came 10 years of Congress rule during which the plight of the living was a reflection of the savagery that marked the death of their families. Nobody was brought to justice. The Congress did nothing to right the wrongs of the BJP, much less its own.

One common feature of all these tragedies is that the Administration aids and abets the crime and no criminal is ever brought to book when the victim is a Muslim. There is no difference between the Congress and BJP in this respect, except that the Congress was in power for much longer.

As a community, we're a people who spend a thousand times more on ostentatious weddings than on poverty eradication of our own people. We're steeped in Shirk and openly disobey and challenge the orders of Allah. We forget and ignore that the decisions of Allah are based on our actions. We forget that results need investment. We forget that good luck comes to those who are prepared – it is the name for what happens when aspiration meets preparation. We are selfish and concerned only about ourselves – ask when was the last time you saw Muslims agitating because a Dalit was murdered? Ask what we did when Christian priests and nuns were murdered and churches burnt in Orissa. We moan only about our own and watch silently when it happens to others.

We follow leaders who have never even seen a global platform and wouldn't recognize it if it punched them in the eye and have no clue what to do if they're given access. Yet we, the followers, don't have the intelligence to see this or to recognize how suicidal it is to follow such leaders who at best are an embarrassment and a clear symptom of the fatal malaise that we are plagued with - congenital blindness. If one makes a mistake once, it is an opportunity to learn. If he makes the same mistake twice, it's a sign of stupidity. We have made this mistake multiple times.

Our current situation, documented in the Sachar Committee Report, is the result of a complete failure of our leadership at every level. That we have done nothing significant to change that situation, 8 years since the report was published (30 November 2006) apart from carping, is a mark of the fact that we are lethargic, looking for saviors and ripe for the taking as victims of anyone who wants to use us. We have been used and discarded many times, yet we learn nothing. We're in this mess because of our leaders not despite them. Our leadership is self-serving, corrupt, blind and deaf, concerned more about interpersonal conflicts than about the welfare of the community. Our leaders – sadly religious leaders included – are at each other's throats publicly, plunging the common man into confusion about who to follow.

We need leaders with vision and strategy and followers who're willing to put aside differences and unite and work with discipline to achieve the goal of uplifting the community. We're people who can't see the need to invest in developing leaders yet we complain that we don't have good leaders. Leaders don't grow on trees even in 10 Janpath. Until we learn to put our money, time and energy where it counts, we will continue to suffer. So until we get the leaders we need it's better to batten down the hatches and ride out the storm. Following such people will only lead to more grief.

Test: Name one Muslim leader who you'd love to apprentice your son to so that he may become like him.

*"Pity the nation that is full of beliefs and empty of religion.
Pity the nation that wears a cloth it does not weave
and eats a bread it does not harvest.*

*Pity the nation that acclaims the bully as hero,
and that deems the glittering conqueror bountiful.
Pity a nation that despises a passion in its dream,
yet submits in its awakening.*

*Pity the nation that raises not its voice
save when it walks in a funeral,
boasts not except among its ruins,
and will rebel not save when its neck is laid
between the sword and the block.*

*Pity the nation whose statesman is a fox,
whose philosopher is a juggler,
and whose art is the art of patching and mimicking*

*Pity the nation that welcomes its new ruler with trumpeting,
and farewells him with hooting,
only to welcome another with trumpeting again.*

*Pity the nation whose sages are dumb with years
and whose strongmen are yet in the cradle.*

*Pity the nation divided into fragments,
each fragment deeming itself a nation."*

— *Khalil Gibran, The Garden of The Prophet*

Yet we must never lose hope. Not only because it is Allah who we worship and on Whom we rely, but also because those who lose hope perish. For all our faults we have been around for 13 centuries while the BJP government will be around for 5 years. So we must work with hope and with great dedication to improve our situation. Waiting for Avatars to save us is not from our theology. We are a nation which believes in the power of self-help. Let us show it to the world. The time is now.

<u>Make sense of what is happening</u>:

The world has changed. Our leadership has failed spectacularly. Solutions to our problems are not with those who are the cause of those problems. So what we must do is to set up Think Tanks to collect and analyze data and project scenarios. Then we must plan investment for the scenarios we choose to focus on. We live in a connected world and we must learn to use those connections. Simply updating FB statuses doesn't help. We must learn to harness the power of technology to tell the world our story. We need to create Media Watch groups who will monitor what is reported about Muslims and Muslim issues and can counter propaganda effectively. We need to train people in this. We must realize that we need to create a whole new generation to do all this. Our traditional leaders are a part of the problem. Expecting them to give us solutions is unrealistic. If they had solutions we wouldn't be in this mess. I know I am going to be called 'disrespectful,' but someone must tell the emperor that he is naked.

Make Hard Decisions:

Money talks. More money talks more. This election proved the power of money. So we must decide to invest in ourselves – in long term projects to develop global Muslim leaders. We need to put our money where our mouth is. It is a tragedy that in a population of 200 million there is not a single Muslim leader who can represent the case of Indian Muslims at the United Nations, for example. I am not saying that we need to do it today. Just that if we needed to, we have nobody who can do it. Unpleasant as it is, we must recognize this and do something to change this situation.

We must also consciously stand up against divisive leaders. We have spawned too many of those. We need to reject them and support those who speak the language of inclusion. That we have leaders who thought that polarizing the vote was a viable strategy beggars the imagination. We need to keep hearts together and take people along if we want to build unity. And unity is what we need above all else. Unity can't be defined as, 'Let us unite – everyone please agree with me.' Unity must be built by accepting diversity of views and practices. By respecting difference and the right of the other to differ. We need to do this across religions but let us begin with our own people. Sadly, we are most divided amongst ourselves.

We must invest in a Legal Cell to study all legislation tabled in Parliament and act to ensure that the interests of our people are protected and that our Constitutional Rights are not frittered away. The Legal Cell must also pursue justice in all cases where Muslims have been harmed. We support the rule of law but that has to be claimed and pursued for it doesn't always happen automatically as we have learnt all too often to our cost. We must support the education of our youth in the areas of journalism, law and politics to create a cadre of capable workers. We must claim our rights and realize that you never get what you deserve. You get what you can negotiate.

Finally, we must decide to work for the long haul. Our current situation of confusion and weakness didn't happen overnight. Its solution will also take time to show results. We must work for the benefit of the community and the nation – not for the seductive glory of flash bulbs. Those who can't work quietly and steadily and who seek publicity must be rejected. They demonstrate childish immaturity that we can ill afford. We need to work with faith and perseverance. For in the end the race goes to the one who stayed in it long enough.

India Muslims – Looking Ahead

*If you want to be successful, you must respect one rule:
never lie to yourself.*

~ Paulo Coelho

UP elections are over and the results are out. They may seem surprising to those who have become used to living their lives in slumber. But for those who had their eyes open, the result in UP was neither unexpected nor sudden; it was a result of 90 years of dedicated effort by countless people who will remain unknown but whose effort bore fruit beyond their dreams. We Muslims on the other hand, remained content with complaining and begging. The world changed but we remained stuck in a world that no longer exists. UP election result was (or should be) enough to wake us from the deepest slumber so that we learn to deal with the new world in which we find ourselves. Unless we do that, the results will be far worse than what we may imagine.

So, what must be done now that we are faced with this fait accompli?

The principles of resilience are three:

1. Face the brutal facts without mincing words or looking through rose tinted glasses.

2. Identify critical areas of impact and work on them. Not everything is equally important.

3. Make necessary changes no matter how painful.

This is the framework which I am going to try to follow.

The Brutal Facts

BJP won a landslide victory. All the analysts were wrong. More than being divided, the Muslim presence in politics and the way it was portrayed to others, resulted in the Hindu vote getting consolidated behind the BJP. Muslims have become the bogeyman of Indian politics and it appears that the mere presence of a Muslim candidate is enough to bring out the worst fantasies in the minds of others. That none of this is based on fact is not important. Rumors don't need facts to thrive. I am not going to make a long list of all that is wrong with the situation of Muslims today. I think we have the intelligence to see that. I will suffice to say that if we don't wake up and do what needs to be done, no matter how painful, we are going to enter an era of darkness that none of us has faced in living memory. Our fate is quite literally in our own hands.

The truth is not difficult to see but difficult to swallow.
~ Mirza Yawar Baig

Muslims must understand that their development and future in the country is not restricted to government largesse or elections. It is in our hands and depends on the overall sentiment about us as people, as neighbors, as fellow citizens, which today is at an all-time low. I don't say that this is entirely our fault. A lot of it is the result of systematic propaganda against Islam and Muslims which our neighbors believe. However, our inward looking and exclusionist attitudes have facilitated the misunderstandings and stereotypes. When people don't know you personally it is easy to believe the worst about you. This has happened to us and this must change.

Elections apart, we simply have to win the hearts of the person on the street, the person next door and the person sitting next to us at work. If we do that well, then the sentiment will protect us from those who seek to harm us. We need to be seen as beneficial for all people. Incidentally this is what Allahﷻ described to us and our mission – selected for the benefit of people. We need to therefore redefine how we look at ourselves vis-à-vis others and decide what we need to do to change the negative image into a positive one.

"In order to change an existing paradigm, you do not struggle to try and change the problematic model. You

create a new model and make the old one obsolete."   ~
R. Buckminster Fuller

All change is painful. Drastic change is even more painful. But the most painful is annihilation. That is what must be remembered when we want to complain about what I am about to propose. Annihilation, not literally, but in every other way, as productive, influential and important citizens of the country. We are facing a future where when the words of the Constitution are spoken, "We the people of India", 200 million citizens will not be included in the term, 'We the people.' Once again, if that comes to pass, it will be with our active or tacit agreement. Nobody to blame but ourselves.

I believe that there are three areas we must address urgently.

1. Societal impact
2. Approach to religion
3. Political presence

1. <u>Changes for Societal Impact</u>

Become beneficial and be seen as beneficial. The way to the heart is through the belly as they say. This means that people need to feel and taste the goodness of anything to believe it. Words are cheap and today we are looking at a society that has become intensely cynical and has no trust in anyone's words. Action speaks; not just louder than words but it is only actions that speak. People don't care what you say until they see what you do. The change must come within our community. We must shed our exclusivist image and communicate with others (non-Muslims). Talk to your neighbors, colleagues, customers. Just talk. Not talk theology but just normal everyday talk. Help them even if they don't help you. Be good to them even if they are not good to you. Greet them in their terms and thank them for any service; for example, thank the taxi driver, the bus driver, check-in and check-out person, the waiter, the doorman, anyone. Thanking increases blessing and changes hearts. This must be done such that people change their perception about us.

I know this is difficult especially in a society that has become very polarized and Muslims are denied housing and jobs. It is difficult but that is why it is even more critical to do it. As for the polarizing society, it is good to remind ourselves that we are equally responsible for it with less justification because polarization is suicide for a minority, yet we did it and allowed it to happen. That is the reason we must change this perception by being genuine and approaching our fellow countrymen and women with love, respect, openness and acceptance. It is critically important to give this message to our children who mirror what they hear at home. Listening to the young ones of all communities tells you a sorry tale about the kind of psychological conditioning that is taking place in our homes. All of us, Hindu, Muslim, Sikh, Esai (Christian) – remember the song?? Today these are empty words. I weep when I recall my own childhood when a friend was simply a friend. His name wasn't a flag to his caste. We lived in each other's homes, ate each other's food, called each other's parents, Amma, Mataji, Dadji, Papa, Baba. Where did we lose it all?

We must set up a fund to create the following institutions open to everyone:

Legal Aid Cell

1. Establish Legal Aid Cells in every city and take up cases of all those who need legal aid – **not only Muslims**
2. Make a list of cases that need to be tackled in order of priority and ease of winning
3. Make Law a primary study focus for students
4. Ensure that no attack on anyone goes unchallenged, because injustice to one is injustice to all

Focus on education

1. Set up high quality English medium schools which teach vocational skills
2. Open them to everyone – **not only Muslims**

3. Make it compulsory for every child to go to these schools until the high school level

4. Make Madrassas only for higher education – graduation and above. Not for primary and secondary education

5. Make every child a potential entrepreneur

Employment

1. Set up a Zero Interest Venture Capital Fund and an Advisory Council to help startups, and open both to everyone – **not only Muslims**

2. Send our youth into the army and police both at officer and serviceman levels. This will inculcate discipline and a sense of belonging to the nation, both of which are missing today

3. Muslim youth must also enter teaching, judiciary, journalism & media professions

4. Zero unemployment is possible with entrepreneurship

Social Development Fund

1. Set up a Social Development Fund to help anyone in need – **not only Muslims**

2. Focus on prisoners who need bail, hospital expenses, clean water, sewage, housing, vocational education, entrepreneurial development, orphans, widows

3. Focus on women's economic and educational development to ensure empowerment of women

4. Demonstrate the real face of Islam to the world of helping everyone to be well

Funding for all the above

1. Central collection of Zakat Funds.
2. Capitalizing of Awqaf (Religious endowments).
3. Voluntary contribution of Rs. 100 per person per month.
4. Additional charitable donations.

2. Approach to religion

Change our ways

The change must begin within us, individually, within our families and within our community. We need to clean up our lives of all forms of disobedience of Allah ﷻ and ensure that we spread goodness all around us. Islam doesn't distinguish between Muslim and non-Muslim when it comes to justice or welfare. Neither must we. Our presence must be seen as a blessing in the community we live in, our cities and villages. This message must be spread by all of us in our different capacities. The major share of this lies on the Ulama who have access to the Friday congregations.

Their message must be about distinguishing ourselves through service, bringing hearts together and against every form of divisive thought, ideology and message. We need to root out the social evils that our society is plagued with, chief among them being alcoholism, gambling and ostentation. Our ostentatious weddings are a case in point. To celebrate weddings the way we do when our own people are as poor and deprived as they are is immoral and criminal. To participate in such functions is to aid and abet the crime.

Not only must we consciously stop propagating differences and divisiveness, but we must vehemently do the opposite. Preach and promote by word and action, inclusiveness, acceptance and brotherhood. Universal brotherhood because that is the way of Islam. Universal brotherhood and forgiveness are values that are unique to Islam. These values must be revived urgently because our lives are currently desolated and deprived of both. Today, not only do we preach divisiveness with respect to non-Muslims, we preach it with respect to Muslims who don't belong to our particular cult, juristic order (Madhab), culture or region. This is completely Haraam. It is not in the scope of this book to quote from the Qur'an and Sunnah to prove my statement but there are plenty of lectures of mine with references that you can listen to.

Secondly, on the national front the following actions must be taken with respect to our Madrassas and the AIMPLB. Our Madrassas are a symbol of great dedication but very poor quality. The result is that graduates are maladjusted and incapable of being productive members of society and are looked down upon and treated with disdain. To change this, we need to change what we teach and how we do it.

Madrassa Education

1. Set up a Central Madrassa Board to ensure the following:
2. All Madrassa teachers must be qualified to teach & have a teaching degree. Our Madrassas are perhaps the only schools where teachers need not be trained to teach. This is so incredibly insane that I feel ashamed to write it.
3. Corporal punishment must be banned and punishable if practiced.
4. Madrassas should be for higher (college) education. Not earlier.
5. Centralized curriculum, syllabus and examination system. Present curriculum and syllabi should be redesigned to make them current, relevant and effective. Please see my paper 'Madrasa Education' (http://yawarbaig.com/2017/03/20/madrassa-education-in-india-what-needs-to-change/).

6. Centralized management of funds by the Madrassa Board so that funds can be allotted to those who need them and not be squandered by those who happen to have the ability to raise them.

7. Transparency in all matters and merit being the only consideration.

8. Establish the Maktab system, local schools that run for a couple of hours every evening, to educate children in Islam. This is very successfully practiced in South Africa, the UK and elsewhere and can be replicated in India.

AIMPLB

1. AIMPLB to abolish triple Talaq and not oppose UCC. Let the government introduce the UCC which will be debated nationally in which we can also participate. No need to say anything until then. The image of being regressive must be changed.

2. AIMPLB membership must be democratized and operations made much more efficient and relevant.

3. AIMPLB to be the sole dispenser of Fatwas on any matter. All random Fatwa dispensers to be stopped.

4. No knee jerk reactions and no working in slow motion.

Subsidies & Reservations

1. Demand that the Hajj Subsidy be abolished. It is a subsidy to Air India, not to Muslims. Refuse to take it. Any travel agent can get us better fares than Air India.

2. Hajj is not Fardh on anyone who can't afford it. We don't need to give our detractors another stick to beat us with.

3. Demand that Hajj Committee be abolished. It gives little benefit and with the removal of the Hajj Subsidy its purpose will vanish.

4. Ditto for all Reservations. We don't need them. Nobody respects beggars. We need to become self-sufficient. Reservations have never solved anyone's problems and they won't solve ours. They are yet one more stick for our detractors to beat us with.

3. <u>Political presence</u>

Leave politics as contestants

UP elections have proved that as things stand Muslim presence in politics as contestants only serves to drive everyone into the arms of the Hindutva brigade. Their absence will enable those who stand for principles instead of caste to have a voice to try to steer Indian politics away from a purely caste-based contest. This may sound drastic but I believe our situation today has reached such a desperate state that we need to consider drastic changes. Like invasive surgery and chemotherapy, even the pain and evil after effects become acceptable when life is at stake. I believe we have reached a stage today where our survival as viable, functioning members of society as Citizens of India seems to be at stake. So we should not stand for election at least for a five-year period. If you are not there, you can't become the bogey man. Muslims must break out of it. We must reject all extremist talk and ideas. Polarization may help some individuals but it is suicide for the community. We must partner and cooperate with all those who stand for justice, human rights, dignity and solidarity of the nation.

Conclusion

I believe the time has come for Indian Muslims to rethink their very existence in this country. We are Indians by choice. We love our country and want to contribute to its development. Therefore, it is time to stop living in isolation and start participating in every aspect of life in our country as CONTRIBUTORS. Not merely whine and complain about negative things that happen to us but do nothing positive to help others. Nobody can harm us – unless we allow it. All this will take time and effort. All this will be painful at least to some. All this needs serious investment of funds. But without it, we will cease to exist as relevant and significant members of this society.

The writing is on the wall. The choice is ours.

Strategic Advice to GOI

The BJP must decide what it is - bird or beast. It must decide what its core ideology is. The BJP and the RSS seem to be confused in this respect and that is a fundamental problem. I am happy to offer a Core Ideology Workshop to them.

Whatever be the historical philosophy of the RSS and its imaginary problems with Muslims, the reality is that every theocracy in today's world has failed. That is because theocracies (no matter what the religion may preach) are based on the principle that people following the state religion are superior human beings and others are inferior. That simply doesn't work and creates so much internal turmoil that the state's major attention and resources become tied down to quelling disturbances. Eventually it fails. Examples abound and so will be the case with a Hindu theocracy, assuming that they can make it happen. I won't even go into the million reasons why that is a pipe dream, speaking from the point of view of Constitutional Law. I am saying that even if they pull it off, it will fail because in today's world, theocracies are outdated and finished.

As for the way they are going about it, they seem to be out of control. They have let loose forces which are not in their own control. I don't believe that someone is sitting at the center of his spider's web directing Operation Lynch. He and others are as clueless about how to control what they have (inadvertently?) started as anyone else. They have to support it as it is being done in their name and so they are supporting it by their silence. But that is a short-term strategy. At some point very soon they will have to take a public stand. Murder remains a crime in this country and can't be ignored forever. If they take a formal stance supporting it (I don't think anyone is that insane) we can imagine what will happen.

Meanwhile, farmer suicides, the two major body blows to the economy – demonetization and GST (BJP fought tooth and nail against it at 18% for a number of years and then brought it in at 28%), the ongoing Maoist civil war, China and Pakistan and the huge unrest (what a nice word to describe another civil war) in Kashmir are real issues which are setting this country on fire. Only a completely insane person or someone who is an enemy of India will contemplate antagonizing another 20 crore Muslims, four times that number of Dalits as well as all the people with different food habits from the currently 'approved', in Goa, North Eastern states, Kerala and AP/Telangana, simultaneously. Remember that all these people were until now living peacefully and many even voted for the BJP. What sense does it make to antagonize them all on something as stupid as what they eat? It is not the job of the government to worry about or try to control what people eat, drink, wear, worship or marry.

It appears to me that this government has fallen into the fatal trap of believing its own PR. It doesn't want to face the harsh reality that demonetization affected the poor, the housewife, the small trader, the person who saved up for years for a rainy day and overnight made them criminals and black-market hoarders, while the big players of the black-market, flew the coop. I would suggest that our national leaders walk into the streets of East Delhi in disguise and talk to the small traders and manufacturers there about demonetization and the second surgical strike on the economy, the GST. I don't say that GST is bad in itself but the way it was implemented has left people shell shocked. Surely that was not so difficult to foresee and mitigate.

I can't believe that people who are educated and intelligent have become so blind as not to see what this is doing to the nation and to their own political future. The complete lack of opposition in this country today leaves the BJP free to make history as one of the best parties to have ruled India in terms of economic development and poverty alleviation; provided it does that and doesn't get side-tracked into a completely negative agenda of religious extremism, crony capitalism and abuse of power.

Remember that in a nation that has no Social Security, National Health Service, State Funded Education or Elderly Care, it was these small businesses that were doing the work of the State at their own expense. Every one of them was taking care of between ten and one hundred people. I am talking about businesses ranging from the Istiri-wala, vegetable vendor, snack carts to one-shop printing presses, lathe machines and cottage industries of all kinds. It is true that many were not under the direct tax umbrella but they all paid taxes in one form or another and what is more important, they took care of their families, relatives, employees and society. They kept the market alive, they fueled commerce, they created a credit flow, they paid for goods and services. They took care of the elderly, the sick, educated their children, paid their bills and were the blood of this nation, which keeps it alive. These were the people who took the biggest hit in both demonetization and while they were still reeling from that blow, the GST. All this while Vijay Mallya still goes to the Oval and Wimbledon.

Individual freedom is the glue that binds a nation. Take that away and the fabric of nationhood unravels. And as the Hindi song goes - even if you join the thread, there will be a knot in it. The job of the government (and the basis of the BJP's election promise) is economic development of the nation. Nothing else. Add to this the responsibilities of public health and education which result in happier, more productive people and economic well-being. Any government that loses sight of this sinks its own ship. America is a classic example today with Trump and his insane policies.

Taxation, money supply, encouraging and supporting entrepreneurship, safety and security of life and property, fair wages and employee benefits and care of children and the elderly must be the focus of the government. This must be visible from every statement made, budget spend, policy formation and implementation and time and energy spend of the leadership; not simply ad-agency inspired PR campaigns. In all these areas, today this government has failed the nation. There is still time to salvage the situation, but it will take above all, political will and a strong leadership stance to do an about-face.

I am aware that allowing the situation to get to where it is today by remaining silent has led to a situation where the leadership is riding a tiger. The longer they stay on its back, the more difficult and costly it will be to get off. Even today, if good sense prevails and the government simply applies the law of the land, reins in the goon squads, punishes the guilty, compensates the aggrieved (difficult though it is to put a price on human life) and makes its position clear both on maintaining law and order as well as economic development, the situation is salvageable. However, we are fast running out of time. And when we do, then only God can save us. In this case we must ask, 'Which God?'

In the words of the great MLK, 'When the truth must be spoken, silence is culpable.'

The Birth of a Narrative

Looking at the headlines it appears that a story is being built – gradually one article at a time; linking one incident to another, using conjecture in the place of hard evidence – to create the new bogeyman – the Indian Muslim as a 'fifth column'. A simple search for the meaning of the term revealed this:

*A **fifth column** is any group of people who undermine a larger group—such as a <u>nation</u> or a <u>besieged city</u>—from within. The activities of a fifth column can be overt or <u>clandestine</u>. Forces gathered in secret can mobilize openly to assist an external attack. This term is also extended to organized actions by military personnel. Clandestine fifth column activities can involve acts of sabotage, disinformation, or espionage executed within defense lines by secret sympathizers with an external force.*

This trend is nothing new of course but it is certainly something that has taken a new energy today from tragic happenings in the Middle East – in particular, the rise of the ISIS – the so-called Islamic State. I say so-called because strangely, or not so strangely, it contradicts every criterion of a true Islamic state, yet it calls itself that. So I gave it another name - Isn't Isn't - it isn't the Islamic State by any stretch of the imagination.

The problem of course is that discourse belongs to those who choose to speak and so those who are silent are to blame if the discourse takes a turn they don't agree with or accept. When the truth must be spoken, silence is culpable. Add to this the problem that some young people who don't understand international politics are falling prey to the ISIS propaganda. In this context, I love Dr. Martin Luther King Jr.'s wonderful reminder:

"Cowardice asks the question - is it safe? Expediency asks the question - is it politic? Vanity asks the question - is it popular? But conscience asks the question - is it right?

And there comes a time when one must take a position that is neither safe, nor politic, nor popular; But one must take it because it is right."

I, as a common man, have the same access to news – papers and TV news – as anyone else. What is clear is anyone who goes by 'official statements' of any political organization or by newspaper or TV headlines, without asking some critical questions, is bound to head off in the wrong direction. If there ever was a time to which the adage, deceptive appearance or wolf in sheep's clothing, could be applied, it is this time. It appears as if all wolves are wearing sheepskin and bleating like lambs while sharpening their fangs for the fatal bite.

So what are the questions that I asked and suggest those who think should ask?

1. How is it that in a world, if you transfer anything over $ 5000 through a perfectly legal bank transaction, you are asked for justification, but the entire ISIS war is being funded by a lot more than $5000 and those funds are not being frozen?

2. How is it that when a single individual who dares to call himself a 'mujahid' is immediately labeled a 'jihadist' and is tracked, arrested and incarcerated, but an entire army is allowed to be recruited and equipped and is allowed to plunder and murder at will and no action is taken?

3. How is it that someone who calls himself Amir-ul-Mumineen – Leader of the Believers – he and his people go against all rules of the Shari'ah and murder innocent Christian and other civilians, kill journalists and non-combatants, shamelessly publish videos of these despicable, Haraam actions, destroy churches, desecrate and destroy tombs of Muslim scholars and even Prophets?

4. Whose interests are really being served to have something like the ISIS operating in that theatre – the interests of Muslims globally or the interests of those who are famous for fighting proxy wars seeking the portraying and labeling of Muslims in highly negative terms?

5.   Finally, how is it that someone who claims to be the Khalifa (Ameer-ul-Mumineen) is silent about the genocide in Gaza? I won't venture to speculate on the reasons. Actions speak far louder than any words possibly can.

The answers to these questions are more than obvious and so we and anyone with any intelligence can only reject the ISIS as being a false flag operation. We reject the ISIS, Boko Haram, Shabab and all other such organizations and condemn their actions and condemn those who play these games at the expense of the lives and blood of innocents. We demand an end to all wars and all games played by the rich and powerful for which the poor and oppressed pay the price. We call upon all intelligent people to use their intelligence and not fall into the propaganda traps being woven to achieve nefarious ends of cynical pitiless people who care for nobody.

As for Indian Muslims and the narrative being created against them – as I mentioned it is nothing new – but if Muslim youth fall into the propaganda trap of ISIS or such organizations and do things which appear to support them, not only will they expose themselves to prosecution, but will also give credence to those who are seeking to label Indian Muslims as less than patriotic and possibly traitors. So we advise anyone who will listen to us to reject anyone who supports the ISIS or any such outfits.

Demanding that Muslims must condemn the ISIS is typical xenophobic and communal nonsense. We don't have to condemn something that we didn't create nor support. Let those who created ISIS condemn it and stop supporting it. Freeze their funding, which will stop them as surely as a hole in the head. Let their creators and funders understand that they are not fooling anyone. We the people of the world and we the Muslims are able to see the schemes behind the events. We are not fooled by the whimpering of captive media who have sold the very spirit of free press and journalism down the drain.

As for us Indian Muslims, we are and have always been Indian first and last. Our religious identity is our personal matter and being Muslim doesn't make us any less Indian than being Hindu makes our Hindu brethren any less Indian. It is a shame that we are always challenged to declare our loyalty. We see this as the demand of vested interests, not the demand of our motherland. India knows us and we know our Watan. This is our country. We love it like all others who live in it. We pray for its safety and prosperity. And we will fight for its integrity. Our history is replete with honor of our contribution to our nation and we are proud of it.

Trump – New Meaning

Whew! Finally, the charade is over. Donald Trump is now the President of the United States of America. What does that mean? It means that the Simpsons prediction came true: https://www.thesun.co.uk/news/2146815/the-simpsons-correctly-predicted-a-donald-trump-presidency-16-years-ago-in-episode-set-in-the-near-future/

So now you know who to refer to for accurate predictions about the future. Goodbye Tarot cards, et al. In 1995, I recall reading a survey which concluded that America was not likely to be ready for a woman president for the next twenty years. Twenty-one years later, it looks like that prediction was true. Given that women in America to this day are paid 80% of what men are paid, it is not surprising that Americans find it tough to visualize a woman in the White House in any place other than the President's bed.

So, what does Trump mean for America, for American Muslims, for Muslims worldwide, for non-whites in America and globally? I am asking this rhetorical question as I see all kinds of doomsday predictions flying around. I apologize for taking a different view. I see the Trump presidency as an opportunity for those who believe in the opposite of everything that Donald Trump promoted in his campaign to put their actions where their mouths are and show that they are as willing to stand up for their values as he was.

What does Trump mean for America? I hope he will be the best thing that ever happened to America. I hope that he can truly make 'America Great Again'. I say that because though I am not American (should I say, 'Thank God?'), I am one who believes that a truly 'Great America' can make this world great. The world truly needs to change. We need someone to lead the way to make the world compassionate, caring, to lead the fight against injustice, corruption and poverty, against disease and ignorance. Which nation is better suited to lead that fight? America has the resources, the intelligence, the education and the leadership ability which I hope it chooses to exercise. Trump won on the anti-establishment platform. I support that fully. The establishment has shown that what it can do is fail spectacularly. The economy crashed and Obama rewarded those who crashed it. People were and are homeless when there are empty homes on foreclosed loans enough for every American to have two homes, not only one. Yet they are on the streets. I hope Trump can put Americans back in their own homes.

Bush, father and son, started never ending wars. Obama continued them adding his own flavor of drone strikes – using technology to create bug splats (the arrogance is incredible) – thereby escalating the global threat level that comes from driving people to desperation. Obama's dabbling (what else to call it?) in Middle Eastern politics resulted in continuing the misery for people of Afghanistan and Iraq and new misery for people of Syria and by inference, the rest of the world. And to top it all, ISIS came into being due to all of the above. The credit can be shared by all of them. So, Trump standing against the establishment, means that he is against all of this. I sincerely hope so.

All the jingoism that he rode on will be diminished when it comes to facing reality. It is easy to talk about kicking out the Mexicans and so on. But the day he does that, reality will dawn on him and his cohorts like it did on those who voted Pro-Brexit; that the rich need the poor to survive while the poor don't need the rich. When nice white Americans get to pay $3 per potato, they will realize the value of cheap labor. Meanwhile, some contractor will get the contract to build the Wall, which he will do from the Mexican side, no doubt as otherwise his margin will not make it worthwhile. So also, the wonderful idea to outlaw the H-1 visa. I don't think it will take very long for Trump and his gang to realize that there is a reason there are blond jokes. And that Indians are not blond. Go figure that.

The good news is that Trump made public what was private - racism, misogyny in a country that never stops 'trumpeting' about women's equality, support for genocide, wars and weapons sales, the evils of unbridled capitalism, locker-room conversations which indicate attitudes - have all come out of the closet and locker-room. Now it is up to those who like to say that they believe in the opposite of all these things, to get off their backsides and bring about change. They can no longer live the lives of pretense and lies that they had become used to, saying, 'It is not happening here.' Trump proved that it is happening and has trumpeted it from the top of Trump tower. Sorry for so much bad punning in one breath. But there you go.

As for Muslims and Trump, believe me Trump is far better than what Muslims have seen in the past. He is far better than what we have today. Take Sisi, the Oily royals who are personal friends of every weapons dealer, the Paki leadership and I can think of several more and Trump begins to look like a choir boy. What will he do that is not already happening? Frankly I don't know and don't care to speculate because the prime movers behind Muslim affairs are Muslims themselves, our Muslim leadership, or more correctly its spectacular failure. Ordinary citizens pay the price, but what's new about that? The fact remains that until we sort that out and do something about taking charge of our destiny, we must remain satisfied with others writing the script we are compelled to live by. Play endings depend on the script, not on the players.

India is a classic example where a so-called minority of 200 million is kicked around like a football and used at will by every mercenary politician for his own ends. But Indian Muslims seem to be satisfied with that, so who is anyone else to complain. If you disagree and tell me that they are not satisfied, then I must ask you what it is that prevents them from doing what is glaringly obvious; get their act together, change their leaders and write their own script. 200 million is not a minority. It is a nation. But only if it chooses to be. Same story for Muslims globally. No point in blaming Trump or looking up to him to find solutions. It is our problem and we must solve it, so let us start doing that.

Two other points: what about wars, global warming and such issues? Well, when you have a nation that lives on perpetual warfare and is supported in that by all the other major industrial nations who either manufacture and sell weapons or buy them, how can you pin it all on Trump? If weapons are made and sold, there will be wars. Wars will continue if they are profitable for those who run them. That people die seems inconsequential because those at the top, who laugh all the way to the bank, don't. Those that die don't seem to count. They are 'collateral', necessary to prove the efficacy of the weapons that were used to vaporize them. If it wasn't for the bugs who splatted, how would you assess the drones or their operators? The fact that the bugs were innocent or that they had families—well, bugs are bugs. And that's all that there is to it.

Global warming? America decided on that when it chose Bush instead of Al Gore. For a minute I thought that was because they got confused because his name is Al Gore like Al Ghurair. But then I realized that it was because he had a terminal problem; he had a brain. See his famous movie, An Inconvenient Truth, and you will see what I mean. https://www.algore.com/library/an-inconvenient-truth-dvd If you do nothing else, buy this and see it. At least you will know why you died. Since you chose that, especially Americans, I believe it is only fair that you understand what you did. With Trump, that came out in the open, so get used to summer all year long. You won't need to go to the French Riviera for a tan. You can get it at home. That is not inconvenient.

Add to this the effect of unending wars, refugee movement, changing cultures, security nightmares coming true, widening gap between the rich and the poor, global poverty and hunger, preventable disease which is not prevented because there's no profit in it – when I think about all this and Trump's election, Nero comes to mind. Renewing our link with tradition. Let us dance to the tune. What's the use of fiddling otherwise?

Final question that everyone is asking, 'How safe is it to have someone like Trump with his finger on the nuclear button?'

My answer is, 'The one who actually pressed that button was as different from Trump as could be. Yet he did it.' Let me leave you to figure out the rest.

Meanwhile, it is midnight where I live, far away from Trump and America and time to go to bed. Truly it is said that there is solace in sleep. So, good night, world. Sleep well. As long as you stay asleep you can escape responsibility.

If I Advised the AIMPLB

I want to begin with a brief thumbnail view at global geopolitics since the collapse of the Soviet Union under President Gorbachev. This was an event that was widely applauded and rejoiced, including by Muslims worldwide. Little did they realize what it would lead to. For a military state, an economy based on war, an enemy is essential. When the Soviet Union decided to call it a day with playing sparring partner, the Military Industrial Complex (MIC) needed someone else to justify its existence and to continue to make money for those who run it. It is important to understand that the political entities we call nation states are incidental in this scheme of things. The people who run the show are not bound by any nationality. They are truly global in that they operate from anywhere and across all national boundaries. Laws that bind us and monitor our transactions don't bind these people. This world is run by a handful of men, not countries and politicians. That is why I am not naming any country; not because of any reticence to do so.

In their search, or I should say, as per their plan, they chose Global Islam (GI). I am coining that phrase to differentiate it from Islam as a religion. The religion of Islam is of no interest to MIC. What is of interest is the ability to take GI and project it in the space of the 'Other', which is critical to continued success even survival of the MIC. GI was ideal because it satisfied all the criteria necessary for an effective 'Other', which are:

1. Mysterious: So that all kinds of lies can be attributed to it with impunity
2. Different: 'They' are not white, not European/American, not Christian
3. History: Bad memories of having been defeated by 'them' in the Crusades as well as 'they' having been the only opponent worthy of the name to European royalty and the Church for centuries
4. Ineffective globally: I don't think this even needs an explanation
5. Compliant internal leadership: Well, since they were placed there by MIC and remain on their seats at MIC's pleasure, what choice do they have?
6. Immunity: If they are attacked, killed, countries destroyed, it is no skin off our nose
7. Nebulous: No specific state for one to be accused of aggression. A nebulous cloud called by whatever name seems fit, Axis of Evil, Islamic Terror etc. So, attacking it is easy and no single or group of states can protest in the UN.

8. Polarization: Is easy for all the reasons above and language was invented to legitimize invasion, murder and plunder.

9. Internal conflict: They are divided amongst themselves and prone to being instigated against one another, so very susceptible to manipulation.

In the words of Fredrick Bastiat, "When plunder becomes a way of life for a group of people living together in society, they create for themselves in the course of time, a legal system that authorizes it and a moral code that glorifies it." That is precisely what is happening today in the world and the Muslims are caught in the middle in the proverbial place between a rock and a hard place. There is an old adage, 'Give a dog a bad name and hang him.' It means that the poor dog didn't do anything to be hanged but was the victim of a media campaign against him. Dogophobia got him and he was hanged. That is what those who spend their time and money behind demonizing Islam seem to want to do. Islamophobia is a multibillion dollar industry which like the pre-World War II, anti-Semitism of Germany and Europe is run by those who are trying to make hay while the sun shines.

That is how the deaths of over a million civilians (plus half a million children under the age of ten) in the Iraq war is brushed aside, even though the entire war was based on lies. The massacre of civilians in Bosnia is a post script, the occupation of Palestine and the daily atrocities being heaped on the heads of an imprisoned population are acceptable and the ongoing genocide of the Rohingya people is not worthy of mention. These and many other instances of mass murder, carried out by the MIC military directly or their proxies, which I have not bothered to mention as my point is made, have only one thing in common; i.e. the victims are all Muslim. The mainstream media is the thought steering tool for the great unwashed and ignorant multitude which gets its knowledge exclusively from the TV screen. They are brainwashed to believe that when a Muslim (or many Muslims) dies, he had it coming. But if he fights back, he is an insurgent, terrorist and embodiment of evil.

They don't have the intelligence to ask how a man fighting an occupying army for the right to live in his own home can be an insurgent? This is like the British judge, sitting in judgment on the last Moghul Emperor Bahadur Shah Zafar who had no answer when the King asked him by what right he was being judged by a foreign occupier in his own land. But when you are on the right end of a gun and the other on its wrong end, you can get away with anything, so Bahadur Shah Zafar was banished from his own land and his sons and grandsons were executed. Why? Because they were his sons and grandsons and the British believed in tying all loose ends. Same logic in Iraq, Palestine, Afghanistan and through proxies in Saudi Arabia, Egypt and many other places today. The same logic drove Vietnam and the deaths of hundreds of thousands of Vietnamese at the hands of invaders, French and American.

I wonder how many Americans know the meaning of the term 'Double Veteran'.
http://www.countercurrents.org/2017/10/02/american-rape-of-vietnamese-women-was-considered-standard-operating-procedure/

Rape of Vietnamese women by US troops "took place on such a large scale that many veterans considered it standard operating procedure." It was "systematic and collective"; an "unofficial military policy". One soldier termed it a "mass military policy." Indeed, rape followed by murder of Vietnamese women was "so common that American soldiers had a special term for the soldiers who committed the acts in conjunction: a double veteran". Legitimizing of atrocity is a natural result of the process of dehumanizing the 'other' and believing that they are 'vermin' to 'exterminate' whom is the noble duty of the 'brave and virtuous'.

In support of my contention I quote an article about the Jewish Holocaust which captures the entire process very well. It is a matter of wonder to this day, how the people of Germany not only watched in silence as 6 million Jewish and other people were systematically murdered, but helped in the process by constructing gas chambers, transportation systems and all manner of horrific methodologies which I will leave you to read about on your own.

https://britscript.wordpress.com/2015/01/27/holocaust-memorial-day-the-10-stages-of-genocide/

I never tire of quoting Pastor Niemöller's words about this, which exhort us to stand up before it is too late. Today the world is once again sitting in silence while the MIC juggernaut rolls on; not asking key questions that must be asked, not taking powerful stances for justice, imagining that by doing so, they are saving themselves.

As Pastor Niemöller says, that is what the Germans also thought, until at the end of the war, they contemplated their own devastated cities, lives and homes. Payment always comes.

Martin Niemöller

(14 January 1892 – 6 March 1984)

First, they came for the Communists, and I did not speak out,

because I was not a Communist. Then they came for the Trade Unionists, and I did not speak out, because I was not a Trade Unionist. Then they came for the Jews, and I did not speak out, because I was not a Jew. Then they came for me and there was no one left to speak for me

This narrative of the 'Other' has today, legitimized any kind of atrocity as long as it is done to Muslims and has made hatred of Muslims acceptable everywhere. Just like it had legitimized every atrocity against the Jews in the last century and the Vietnamese (communists) in the 60's and 70's. It is necessary to see the signs and recognize them for what they are and not allow ourselves to be fooled by these age-old games.

That is why in India when a twelve-year-old Muslim boy is stabbed multiple times and killed in a train before his own younger brother, the entire carriage load of people looked on and cheer the murderers. Ask them what the crime of the boy was. Ask them if the boy had harmed them. Ask them why they did nothing. All these questions have only one answer; he was a Muslim. And so, all these things become legitimate and acceptable. In Myanmar, the Rohingya people are being systematically slaughtered, raped and burned alive by the Burmese army and the world watches in silence.

In India once again, in a gathering of upper class, educated people one man, on the topic of the Rohingya genocide, says that what is happening is acceptable and should happen. 'Muslims need to be killed', he says. Nobody protests. Nobody is shocked. Nobody is outraged. One person, not a Muslim, raises a voice protesting, asking if one should not be compassionate; asking if murder is not a crime, no matter who does it. No to all of the above because they are "MUSLIM". What's wrong with you? Why can't you understand this simple fact? I can quote many more examples but I think this is enough. After all we all read the same papers and watch the same channels.

As you can see the narrative needs to be changed. But since that is linked to the well-being of the MIC, how can we, garden variety common people, do it? I am going to attempt to put down my thoughts about what I believe needs to be done for three reasons:

1. I will not allow what is not in my control to prevent me from doing what is in my control. I can't influence the global narrative (or at least I don't know how to do it at

this point) but I can influence the local one, so I am going to try that and share my thoughts with you.

2. No matter what the spin doctors want us to believe, the rule of the MIC can only result in more and more misery for common people, less and less safety and security for us and more and more hatred in society, all in order to make the 1% ever wealthier.

3. No matter how powerful the Dons of the MIC think they are, ultimately their power depends on those who follow them. Without the unquestioning obedience of their followers, they are powerless. That is the reason we must ask questions; uncomfortable questions. Be it about climate change or about global dominance. That is why they spend a colossal fortune on mind steering through the media, films, social media and other means of communication. If George Bush and his gang were really powerful they would have been able to invade Iraq without telling a barrage of lies to the UN and the whole world, first. And if those who listened to the lies had asked the right questions, two million people would have lived. It is as important as that, to ask the right questions at the right time.

Please see my article for more on the need to accept our autonomy and understand that ultimately each one of us is personally accountable. The reality is that unless we decide to believe the false narrative and fall into its trap, nobody can force us into it.

https://medium.com/@yawarbaig/its-not-my-fault-dbc59b7e2712

A couple of questions that you may like to ask, even today:

1. When Saudi Arabia is being held complicit enough in the 9/11 bombing incident for the US Congress to pass the 9/11 Lawsuit Bill, permitting victims to file suits against them, why did President Donald Trump sign an agreement to supply them with $110 billion worth of arms?

   https://www.wsj.com/articles/congresss-passage-of-9-11-lawsuit-bill-marks-new-blow-to-u-s-saudi-relations-1475183243

   https://www.cnbc.com/2017/05/20/us-saudi-arabia-seal-weapons-deal-worth-nearly-110-billion-as-trump-begins-visit.html

2. If ISIS is really so bad, then how is it that despite the overwhelming presence of the US and Allied forces in that theatre, ISIS continues to have an uninterrupted supply of weapons and ordnance, fuel and supplies and cash funds? After all, if you tried to transfer $10,000 to Iraq or Syria, you would have everyone from the IRS to

FBI to your neighbor's dog, breathing down your neck. But there appears to be no problem with billions of dollars being freely transferred and payments for arms and ammunition being credited when it comes to the ISIS. So, who is the enemy and who is the friend?

I am sure you have all read the famous poem "The Charge of the Light Brigade" an 1854 narrative poem by Alfred, Lord Tennyson about the Charge of the Light Brigade at the Battle of Balaclava during the Crimean War and its very famous line: "Ours is not to question why, ours is to do and die." This is the philosophy that keeps hatred of the 'Other' alive, enables genocide, sacrifices the poor and empowers the 1% to remain secure and become wealthier.

Imagine a world where the soldier questions why he is being ordered to kill innocent people. Imagine a world where the person manufacturing weapons of mass destruction questions what value he is adding to society by working in such a place and what legacy he is leaving behind for his family. Imagine a world where people manufacturing cigarettes and alcohol see films on lung cancer and alcohol related car crashes and then make a choice whether to go to work or not. I can imagine more scenarios but will instead leave you to do this on your own. Sit with your children and make a game of it. Imagine a world without war. Imagine a world without the 1% but instead with their wealth shared by those who share the dream of global prosperity. Not global dominance by military might. Wars happen for one reason only and that is because they make profit. Take that away and you would have taken away the reason for war. That is the road to peace. Not attempting to silence all opposition to the dominance of the 1%.

If you are ready to sacrifice your life and happiness to put more caviar and champagne on the tables of the 1%, go ahead but count me out. I want a world where my family, friends and I are safe, can live peacefully together, earn a decent living and leave behind a legacy for the next generation. If you don't like this idea, then you should stop reading this right away. We don't live in little compartments in this world. We live in a world connected in far more powerful and meaningful ways than social media. This doesn't simply mean that we can go from place to place faster or communicate across great distances instantaneously but that what happens to one, affects everyone. The Butterfly Effect of Chaos Theory is not restricted to weather. It affects us in all aspects of life. Those who refuse to recognize it and insist on living as if they live alone in the world, will become its victims.

http://fractalfoundation.org/resources/what-is-chaos-theory/

It's time for all butterflies to start flapping their wings to create a hurricane of world opinion that will drive out all injustice and oppression, no matter where it may be.

Dilemma of the Revolutionary

This is a thought-share primarily for South African leadership who may be interested in an outsider's view of the changes happening in their country. I have taken the liberty of adding my comments on what I believe will be helpful to do. I am not preaching to anyone. This is merely a thought-share with anyone who is interested.

When I graduated in Political Science in 1975, I never thought that I would live in a world where I would actually be able to see almost everything I studied and some more, happening. My world was a stable place with little change, yet poised to take the dive from there into the maelstrom of change that we have become so familiar with today. And it happened in less than two decades.

I was in South Africa last week on my pilgrimage as I like to call my visit to Kruger National Park, truly one of the most beautiful places on earth. As always I also met my old friends, made new ones and watched with interest the changes since my last visit which in this case was in 2014. I have always maintained that there is much for South African leadership to learn from the post-independence history of India, which has the benefit of learning without the pain of actually repeating that history in their own post-independence development. This article is to help those who are interested to do that.

India also came out of its colonial slavery, though without bloody revolution. We shall not mention the fact that we made up for the bloodletting during partition and the formation of Pakistan. The new leaders, Nehru and gang, who took over from the British White Sahib Bosses faced the same post revolution dilemma – how to make the dream you sold to the people come true.

The Indian National Congress headed by Pandit Jawaharlal Nehru as Prime Minister, 'solved' the problems of job creation and land distribution by creating huge Public Sector Organizations run by bureaucrats who knew as much about running a commercial operation as I know about flying a plane. The purpose was to create jobs, not manufacturing efficiency, quality or innovation. And that purpose was achieved by employing at least three people to do the job of one. Worker friendly legislation made it a crime even to frown at a worker who didn't – hold your breath – work. Trade unions became very strong, backed the political party which made the rules and later became the arbiters of power themselves. As long as nobody asked questions about efficiency, productivity, quality or profitability this completely impossible system continued and Nehru and his successors were able to 'show' how they were delivering on the promises made during the Independence Struggle. Nobody asked, 'How long can this continue?' It didn't, as we shall see.

Land distribution was also handled in the same way through legislation which abolished the Zamindari system (feudal system where one person owned the land which was tilled by tenant farmers who were in many, if not most cases, bonded laborers) and introduced the Land Ceiling Act. What happened was that large land holdings were divided up into small plots and given away to the tiller. Sounds so nice and cuddly but with it came the problem that the small owner – the erstwhile tiller – had neither the capital for inputs nor the knowhow for cultivation. He had been a poorly paid worker who did what he was told. Suddenly he became a land owner. So two things happened: 1) Land which had been previously cultivated and yielded good crops, lay fallow and barren and the new 'land owner' went to work on a construction site in a city as a manual laborer since that was the only marketable 'skill' he had. 2) Those new 'land owners' who remained, went back to the old owners and handed in their papers and said, 'Please give me my job back and you can have the land.' So officially they remained owners on paper. But the old status quo of the land owner returned. Militancy also came into being with some of the newly liberated bonded laborers wanting to keep their land and till it. Old owners tried to throw them out with the help of the police and the Naxalite Movement was born. https://en.wikipedia.org/wiki/Naxalite

On the industrial front, Public Sector Corporations reached their size of self-implosion and simply got too unprofitable to run. Government ran out of money to pay salaries and mandatory increments. Labor laws originally created to protect the worker became means of encouraging non-productive behavior. Unions went over the top and in states likes Kerala and West Bengal literally paralyzed business and industry. Voting-in another party did nothing to change the situation. Finally, Government brought in what they called 'Liberalization' – liberating themselves from their false promises. The back of the trade union movement was broken. Today there are no unions in the entire IT and ITES industry in India. Privatization of many areas took place. Manufacturing became more efficient but the ranks of the unemployed increased. In India what helped was the intrinsic entrepreneurial nature of the Indian which resulted in a lot of small and medium enterprise happening all over. Credit became easier to get with nationalization of banks. And the strong family system helped to keep people alive and kicking.

Huge numbers of Indians went to work in Gulf countries and their inward remittances supported their families.

Indians by nature are fatalistic and not militant and so no major public unrest happened, though public misery is all too visible. We're far from being out of the woods because we are now going on the track of fast becoming an oligarchy – with too many millionaires and too many poor people. And the future looks bleak, especially for the poor.

Naxalite militancy is on the increase though not in cities yet. Crime is rampant, though since the media is the mouthpiece of the establishment, it goes unreported. Rampant farmer suicides are one major indicator of a very sick society. Corruption at an unprecedented scale is another. From being something that existed quietly and was indulged in clandestinely, corruption is now an aspirational goal, indulged in totally without shame. The industrialist – politician – bureaucrat nexus is working very well to corner resources for the few at the expense of the many. Fear rules and life is cheap and easily lost.

India is a notoriously corrupt country, with Transparency International giving it a rank of 76/168 (USA is 16/168) where crony capitalism thrives (On the World Bank Groups "ease of doing business index", India is 130/168 and the USA is 7/168) and where inequality reins with extreme poverty (GINI index of 33.9, along with a HDI rank of 135/168). India is also a thriving democracy. All of these things combine into the one

But India is a big country and as they say, 'Even a dead elephant weighs five tons.' So the effects of all this are not yet crippling. But we are getting there.

In 1995 I went to South Africa soon after they won independence, but the only black people I saw were the waiters in my hotel and the servants in the houses of white people, who invited me to a braai. I stood on the viewing deck at the top of the Sun in Sandton at night, the city bright with lights except one big black hole in the distance. I asked someone if there was a power outage. The white man smirked and said, 'This is not India. We don't have power outages. That is Soweto. They have no power.' Very interesting, I thought – arrogance apart. In India we have power outages and still do double digit growth, while in Apartheid South Africa, not giving power to the majority of citizens was state policy.

I went back to South Africa in 2005 and since then have been going there almost annually for my 'pilgrimage' to the Kruger National Park, a journey of love which I look forward to for the eleven months that separate one from the next. I also meet lots of people, businessmen (have I met any businesswomen?), politicians, academics, educationists, farmers, doctors and other professionals, game rangers, students, professors (aren't they academics?); Blacks, Whites, Indian, Colored, Christian, Muslim, Jewish, Atheist, Agnostic, Hindu, I-don't-know-what-I-am; you name it and I've met it. They talk and I listen. I talk of course and sometimes they don't like what I have to say but that is the risk of being an analyst – distance gives perspective, but people who are close to the ground, who don't like the diagnosis you give them, say, 'You don't live here. You don't understand our reality'. Forgetting that it is precisely for that reason – because I don't live in South Africa – that I can see and understand the reality of what is going on.

As I have said before, it is cheaper to learn from others' mistakes than to make your own. South Africa is in the unique position to learn from the mistakes of India but seems unable or unwilling to do so. I have been trying to convince all those I speak to when I visit there to study post-independence India and learn lessons to apply in post-independence South Africa. They all listen respectfully, agree with me entirely about the need to learn, feed me great food, take me to Kruger Park, I put on weight and come home. Nothing changes. I love the hospitality of course and thank my hosts but remind them that I can afford my meals and didn't go there for free food. If they don't change their ways, then I shudder to think about what will happen. And I can't stop that from happening. There are enough examples in Africa itself to look at.

So what is going on in South Africa? A revolution is taking place. It is in progress. It is happening as we speak. But it is a revolution without formal leadership, without clear ideology, without a strategic game plan. It is a revolution of nature. Of human nature to do what it considers best for its own survival, without sometime bothering about any long term results of precipitate action. It is very dangerous.

'Ha! Wrong again', you say. 'Our revolution ended in 1995 when we became free of the apartheid regime. Now it is payment time.'

'No', I gently remind you. '1995 was the first stage in that revolution to become free. You reached that step. The revolution continues and depending on what you do, it can make you truly free or enslave you once again.' The choice is yours. I am the analyst, remember? Also remember, shooting the messenger doesn't turn bad news into good. South Africa is poised on the brink. It can become a case study of what to do or what not to do. It is your choice.

Let me talk some theory first – Revolution 101.

Oppression is oppressive and sows the seeds of its own destruction at its inception. Those seeds germinate in thoughts of freedom. Grow in the atmosphere of yearning for freedom seeing others becoming free. Are watered with the blood of martyrs. Martyrs die and more are needed so those running the revolution have to sell a dream. A dream where in effect the oppressed get everything the oppressors have today. Streets paved with gold, big cars, bigger homes, jobs for everyone, food galore. As the lyrics of the song go, 'Money for nothing and the chicks for free.'

Nobody asks the real question, 'How likely is all this?' Nobody asks and nobody cares, because dreams are supposed to be unrealistic. And let's face it, if it was not attractive enough, why would I leave my family to go and die in the street? I didn't go to die. But I went and I died. And that was some more irrigation for the dream to grow.

Finally, it comes true. We are free. Now what?

Now I am waiting for my job, new car, home, food, 24-hour power supply, clean water, hospitals – you name it and I want it. But it doesn't come. Why not? Because the dream was a dream and dreams have an inconvenient way of coming true with strings attached. But nobody told me that. Well, let's face it. If someone told you that you would have all of the above and more but that it would take two generations of hard work to get it, would you have fought to throw off apartheid? If someone had told you that you would have to go to school and college, study very hard, compete for jobs like everyone in every other country does, would you have died to give others a chance at that? If someone had told you that there's no free meal and no pot of gold at the end of the rainbow, would you have endured the suffering of the revolution? But that is the reality. Like it or not. So the chickens do come home to roost. The promises have to be fulfilled. People will hold you to them, Mr. Revolutionary Leader. And you can't say, 'They are not realistic.' Because you made those promises and at that time you didn't tell me that they were not realistic. You sold the dream. Now deliver. Or help me understand what to do to get it.

Every revolutionary party faces this. The let-down at the end of the revolution, when you expect to be in a permanent state of high in your dreamland come true. But instead face disillusionment, disappointment and even despair. This is the crucial threshold that all political parties who run revolutions have to face and cross if they want to succeed and actually give the people the beautiful life they promised them.

If this is not done, what's the next step in this cycle?

Another party arises and sells another dream. 'We will give you everything that these liars promised and failed to deliver. Jobs, electricity, water, homes, cars, everything. And you need do nothing except to support us. Support us and you will have it all.' And believe it or not, people are ready to believe this story once again. They don't ask the crucial question which they should have asked in the first place – "HOW?" And the cycle repeats. Until of course one day you get a new leader who decides that he can't really give people what they want but also doesn't want to give up power and so a new dictator is born. There are plenty of examples of this in Africa itself – Uganda under Idi Amin for example and others which I am sure I don't need to name.

In our world that is characterized by rapid change, you don't have to go that far back to see this cycle come full circle. Look at Egypt. As they say, 'Power corrupts. Absolute power corrupts absolutely.' Hosni Mubarak was oppressive to put it politely, for decades. Then came Morsi and the Ikhwaan. They sold the dream of freedom, jobs, food and won an election that nobody thought they would win. But once again the people were not prepared to face the reality, that it is not magic. Everything will happen but not overnight. I was in Cairo and Marsa Alam in April and May that year and saw people sitting in roadside cafes, drinking tea and discussing politics. I knew this was a very ominous sign. Disgruntled people with real woes, sitting around in tea shops or bars talking politics in a free country is always dangerous. Sadly, my fears came true and Morsi's government fell and Sisi came to power; even more oppressive than Mubarak. Circle is complete. The future is bleak.

Another good illustration of this process is that of growing up from childhood. A small child is dependent entirely on its parents. So it ascribes all its life experiences to them. If it is happy, parents are good. If it is unhappy, it is the fault of the parents. To an extent this is correct because parents have power and the child doesn't. However, when the child grows up, this equation changes. Parents are no longer powerful or even present. However, many people fail to grow up mentally and simply transfer this attitude of 'Someone else is responsible for my happiness', to their spouses or bosses and go through life blaming others for whatever happens to them. True growing up is to own responsibility for yourself. Not merely to grow facial hair or other indicators of physical maturity. Real maturity is when the individual takes charge of his or her own life and says, 'This is my life and I am responsible and I will do what it takes to make it the most productive and beautiful life possible.' Only then is the person truly grown up and not simply a 30 or 40-year-old child. And this transformation can happen at any age. Not only at 30 or 40.

The same is the case with countries that are under the yoke of oppression. People get used to being powerless and to blaming the ruling class for their problems. As in the case of the child, this is true because they are powerless. But oppression fuels rebellion so some take ownership for this powerlessness and decide to change it and the revolution is born. But what happens is that in the heat of the struggle, nothing is done to enable others to grow up also. And so when independence is won, others merely view the new leaders in the same role as the old – i.e. ruling class – and look up to them in the same way – they are responsible for my happiness. Same chairs, different bottoms. This is dangerous for the 'ruling' party especially as they will be held responsible for the dream not coming true. And the cycle which I mentioned above happens.

Nobody tells the people that there is no 'ruling class' now. That they are the rulers. So if they don't like something they have to change it. They can't any longer blame someone else. They have to collaborate with government to make it productive. Not cop out and sulk or attempt to run away. There is nowhere to run. One can't really run away from oneself, can one? Same logic.

This is exactly what is happening in South Africa today. It is all too visible. Hubris at the success of the struggle. Like kids in a toy shop filling the pockets with all the toys you can get your hands on. Forgetting that now you own the shop and so you can't steal from yourself. You can only harm yourself by filling your pockets. Meanwhile the people who followed you are still used to the 'ruling class' attitude. Nobody told them that there is no ruling class any longer. They are the rulers and so they get to carry the can. They supported you in the revolution – they believed that they were working for you, not themselves. They believed your sales talk about what they would get when they won the revolution. You forgot to tell them that it would take time, investment, sacrifice, hard work and still more time. So they are now waiting to get it.

"I am entitled to it. So give it to me."

"Work? I already did that. I fought in the revolution (or my father or grandfather did) and so I am entitled to the candy. Where is it?"

"On top of that, I see the toys you put into your pocket. I see the candy (corruption, privilege) that you are eating. So why can't I also eat it?"

But enough of diagnosis. Let us look at solutions.

Two things:

1. Leadership: Put your own house in order.

2. Change the mindset from 'Entitlement to Contribution.'

Here's a more detailed explanation:

1. Put your own house in order:

Take the candy out of your pocket and put it back on the shelf. And apologize for taking it out of turn. Help your friends also to do that. The sooner this is done the easier and less painful it is. Delay is suicidal. Corruption is a cancer that is infectious and kills as surely as the real thing. You have to look after your cow. You can't milk it and not feed it. You can't cut out a piece of meat because you are hungry. The cow will die and you will die with it. Corruption is suicide. Root it out ruthlessly and quickly, needless to say, starting at the top. If the head is sick the body can't be healthy. So do whatever it takes to cure the sickness. Swallow bitter pills, perform surgery, cut out the cancer before it kills you.

Tackle crime urgently. Investigate, prosecute and sentence. Sayings like, 'South Africa's national sport is rape', are not funny and indicate an immense sickness.

Year	Sexual Offences	Murder	Robbery
2015	53,617	17,805	54, 927

2014	62,267	16,914	53,424
2013	66,197	16,211	53, 439
Cumulative since 2004	7,83,687	2,12,312	7,83,680

<http://www.crimestatssa.com/national.php>

The figures are horrific and I can perhaps safely say that the victims don't include a single politician of any hue. It is only poor people who have no protection who die and are raped. More people die violently in South Africa than in many war zones. And remember that it is safe to say that in all these cases the number of crimes actually committed is more than those reported.

I personally know of two cases of major robbery, and one where a person was shot through the leg, that were never reported. The reason, which I was amazed to hear, was that people have no faith in the police. This is a very serious matter, where the citizenry has lost faith in Government. Sad to say that there appears to be very little, if anything done by the Government about it. This is something that sits squarely in the lap of the Government and must be dealt with urgently. If necessary, reinstitute the death penalty. Criminals can't have more human rights than victims.

South Africa's crime is the single biggest deterrent for foreign investment. The apathy of the Government in tackling it is impossible to understand. It appears that there is a high level of collusion between police and criminals without which such levels of crime would be impossible.

The second biggest deterrent for foreign investment is the general lack of skills, the result of a failed education system. This again is something that is critical to address and correct without which South Africa will not be able to attract large investors who would be very happy to invest there and set up manufacturing facilities. South Africa needs vocational schools that can train people in marketable skills that can enable them to earn a living. This would directly impact the job market and provide jobs and enhance the quality of life but it can happen only when the country can offer a high level of skills in the workforce. South Africa is the gateway to Africa but at present this seems to be used mostly by the drug trade. Control of crime and drug cartels and a boost in skill development to provide good jobs is the key. I have suggested some ways below.

2. Change the mindset of people from 'Entitlement to Contribution'.

Educate people on the steps forward and show them a realistic plan where they can see how to succeed and taste that success in a reasonable period of time. It is essential that people see results in their main pain areas and see them fast. Government must be seen to be doing things. Saying,

'We won freedom for you', is not enough especially for a generation which didn't see apartheid. This requires the following:

1. The public education system needs major overhauling. That is a subject in itself so I won't talk about it here, except to mention the need to address this urgently. The current system is designed to create failures. It must change.

2. Introduce **Vocational Training** in <u>**all schools**</u>. Every child must learn a trade or skill by the time they complete schooling. That way they will have a marketable skill which they can use to earn a living. It is critical to develop a thriving middle class. Give people something to lose. The problem today is that people have nothing to lose.

3. Rejuvenate the **Farm Schools** and train children in farming while completing their primary, secondary and high school education. Get them connected to the earth. That is the best education and will prepare them for the real thing later. The Afrikaners knew what their Farm Schools produced. Just replicate that and you will get the same results. People connected to the soil are people who are interested in the development of the country.

4. **Ministry of Small Business**: The Right Step Forward – But...

   o It is completely untenable that the Government is the biggest employer in South Africa, employing over 45% of the employed population. No government has the money to pay that salary bill or to take care of inevitable increments, social welfare expenses and so on. There is a critical need in South Africa to create a robust class of self-employed people who not only take care of themselves but provide employment for others.

   o As the sub-heading of this section says, the initiative to set up a Ministery of Small Business is an excellent step. This must be supported and results measured. A good idea is to seek 'Customer feedback' to see how Government's initiatives are being experienced by those for whom they are meant. So listen to people and recruit them in enabling small businesses to succeed.

   o Provide training in all aspects of entrepreneurship. In my view this is the key to development, eradication of crime, handling the food and energy crisis and education in South Africa. Enforce entrepreneurship.

- o Set up a **Venture Capital Fund** to provide prospective entrepreneurs with interest free loans. These must be given after a rigorous selection process of examining business plans and ensuring that they have a high likelihood of success.
- o The capital for this fund can come from major multinational companies operating in South Africa as part of their CSR. I know this is being done by some progressive CEO's but it must be hugely boosted. I believe that the way to do that is by creating a full-fledged Venture Capital Fund that is available to all aspiring entrepreneurs. Business CEO's will recognize the value of such a fund and will fully support it. Invite them to sit on the Board and run it – not government bureaucrats. We need businessmen/women to run this Fund.
- o Pair new entrepreneurs with established businessmen and women who can coach and mentor them.
- o Set up a **National Entrepreneurship University** that trains in all kinds of vocational skills and starting up businesses.

- o Award Prizes for successful startup ventures in all provinces and at the national level. These should be significant monetary awards that encourage people to participate and are worth working for.
- o Institute special prizes for entrepreneurial initiatives in key areas like poverty eradication, alternate energy, education, food production, transportation, health management and other high need areas. Prizes must take into account, innovativeness, social consciousness, creativity.

A vibrant middle class is essential to survival in any economy. The bigger the middle class the bigger the market for goods and services and more money flows into the economy and is available for public services like healthcare, education, transport and so on. Contrary to the myth of trickle down, money doesn't flow down from the superrich or from global multinational corporations into local economies. The superrich don't use local services, live in ivory tower isolation and are generally unaffected by local conditions as they are surrounded by cordons of insulation. Multinational corporations are answerable to their shareholders who don't live in Soweto (so to speak) and so they don't care what happens in local economies. Many don't even employ local people, except in menial jobs because locals may not have the education and skills that they need.

Countries like India and China score over South Africa in this regard because we have a very strong education and skill base and can actually provide potential employers, people of equal competence at a much lower cost. That's not the best USP – buy me because I am cheap – but it works for a while anyway to build a middle class. South Africa has a lot of catching up to do. However, I believe that if the things that I have mentioned above are done urgently, then South Africa will be able to solve its problems of crime, unemployment and political unrest and create a stable, vibrant middle class with a high standard of living.

Close Encounters of the Terminal Kind

Ralph Chaplin said: "Mourn not the dead that in the cool earth lie, but rather mourn the apathetic throng, the coward and the meek who see the world's great anguish and its wrong but dare not speak."

A friend asked me for my opinion about the Bhopal 'encounter' which was in the news. Eight young men, allegedly 'dreaded terrorists', were 'encountered'. This is a cute term invented by the Indian media to describe what should correctly be called 'extra-judicial killings'. And if you are among those who like to reduce everything to a single word, then you may like to experiment with the word, 'Murder'. Truth and facts are boring and don't sell papers or generate TRP ratings for so-called News Channels (which should be called by their real name – Propaganda Machine) but lace the truth with a dash (if required completely drench it) of fantasy, drama, excitement and fear and you can make a jaw-dropping, BP-raising, edge-of-the-seat, breathtaking clip of a cat catching a mouse. That is where the word 'encounter' came into being – murder being rather boring. And those who indulge in it on a regular basis were given the media medal of 'Encounter Specialist'. I will leave you to arrive at what the logical, factual, straight and truthful word is, that should be used..

To give you an example of the monsters our media creates see this headline: http://bit.ly/1eBKIgu Why would anyone fear someone whose specialty is killing innocent, unarmed people? If that is a definition they feel proud of and their law-abiding brethren are not ashamed of, then pray what is the difference between this and the way you would define every daku (dacoit) of Chambal or every supari hitman gangster of the underworld? If honest police officers find such media descriptions insulting, then why do they remain silent? Here's what Wikipedia has to say about 'encounter' killings: http://bit.ly/2eERe9j Let me leave such thoughts to those who should really reflect on them.

I decided to begin at the beginning and googled the term Encounter. Google, like Jeeves, gives satisfaction and so here is what came up.

en·coun·ter
/inˈkoun(t)ər,enˈkoun(t)ər/

verb

1. unexpectedly experience or be faced with (something difficult or hostile).
"we have encountered one small problem"
synonyms. **experience**, **hit**, run into, come up against, **face**, be faced with, confront
"we encountered a slight problem"

noun

1. an unexpected or casual meeting with someone or something.
synonyms: **meeting**, chance meeting
"an unexpected encounter"

Translations, word origin, and more definitions

I am not sure if those who had the encounter (or were 'encountered'; such a useful language, English) would describe what they faced as, *'we encountered a slight problem'*, but fortunately they are not in a position to disagree with this definition, so we can ignore what they may have wanted to say.

So, what really happened in Bhopal?

God, of course, always knows. In this case those it happened to and those who facilitated that happening also know. But one lot is now speechless and the other lot are not speaking. Therefore, I am exactly where all of you are; with an enigmatic mystery to solve. Those addicted to mystery novels (I am, if Jeffery Arthur is the author) will be thrilled that one is unfolding before their eyes. I mentioned JA not by accident but by design. Because one of the most enjoyably infuriating thing about his writing is that the mystery is never completely solved. So, you gnash your teeth in frustration, curse him for being the cussed, devious man he is and wait with baited breath for his next novel, knowing full well that it is going to leave you in the exactly same state. We are all suckers for punishment. That is why I have read all his novels and pray for his long and productive life.

The Bhopal Encounter (it deserves upper case) is a mystery which will never be solved (at least for garden variety lizards like me) and will be followed by another and another as it was preceded by one and more.

Then why write anything at all about it?

I believe the Bhopal Encounter is a snapshot of what happens to democracies and what has been happening to our Indian democracy when those who make up the democracy decide to copout of the process. What defines and differentiates a democracy (India?) from a monarchy (Britain), a dictatorship (Egypt), an oligarchy (USA) or an anarchy (??) is the actions of its people. Democracy is not the name of a system of government. It is the name of a state of being that a nation of people choose for themselves. It is the name of a belief about yourself. It is the name of dignity of the individual. It is the name of justice where the law supersedes the individual (the opposite is the definition of feudalism). It is the name of self-determination, individual liberty, mutual compassion and concern. The system of government called 'Democracy', ensures all this. When its nature changes and it is no longer able to fulfill what the term 'Democracy' defines, it ceases to be a democracy and becomes whatever its actions display, no matter what its PR machine wants to portray to the world. People always see through the covers and know the truth because people listen with their eyes. They don't care what you say, until they see what you do.

Democracy is defined by its three constituent institutions and by their separation; of the law makers, implementers and interpreters. Separation of the Institutions of the Legislature, Executive and Judiciary. "I am the law" or "I am above the law" are both feudalistic statements. The separation is a safety measure to ensure that the democracy always remains a democracy and can't be hijacked to become a dictatorship as we have seen happening all over the world, even though those regimes still call themselves 'democratic', because that is the buzzword to use. After all, how would, 'The Undemocratic, Dictatorial, Fascistic, Murderous, Oppressive, Apartheid Republic of So-and-so' sound? Not nice at all. So, they call themselves 'Democratic', while all the rest are fringe benefits that their citizens enjoy.

The 'Encounter Specialist', by his action (and all those who support that action directly or by remaining silent) collapses the three Institutions of Democracy, where he becomes the lawmaker, the law interpreter and the law enforcer. He decides who is guilty and what the punishment should be. By his action, he declares that mere incidentals like evidence, establishment of guilt, judicial process, criminal code, sentencing and the legal procedure to ensure justice, are all immaterial. He is the judge, jury and executioner rolled into one and by his action, hammers another nail into the coffin of democracy.

The question is not whether the one killed in an 'encounter' was guilty or not. The question is whether justice was done and seen to be done. If we declare that the killing of one by another who considers him guilty is justice, then we have legitimized every terror killing in the world. The man who drove the truck through the crowd in France thought he was doing justice. The person who killed the three Muslim medical students in North Carolina thought he was doing justice. ISIS thinks it is doing justice. Every Israeli soldier shooting Palestinian children thinks he is doing justice. Where do we draw the line, if we choose to obliterate it in one instance?

We either draw the line and say, 'Let the courts decide who is guilty and who is not, based on evidence,' or we open the doors to anarchy and civil war. It is our call. It's the choice of civil society, to raise our voice and say what we want, what we demand from our government, justice or anarchy? The 'Encounter Specialist' represents anarchy. The policeman/woman who investigates a crime and brings the murderer to the gallows represents justice. Whose side are we on? Whose side are you on?

So, who is guilty? Those who commit murder and call it 'encounter', those who order it and all those who sit silently and watch it happen. All of them are equally guilty of destroying the law, destroying the nation and destroying themselves. Especially tragic is when those sworn to uphold the law and protect the innocent are guilty of violating that trust. There's nothing more pathetic than a policeman committing murder at the behest of others. It violates and insults the uniform, the oath of office and the Constitution of India. It is the action of such of them that give a bad name to the entire force, where the term, 'Police Martyrs' sounds like an oxymoron. Those who really lost their lives dishonorably lose the honor they deserve. I remind myself that there are others who I know, who in this morass of shameless pursuit of personal wealth and pleasing political bosses, don't even dream of sacrificing their integrity and stand alone as shining lights proclaiming that honesty and truth are personal values which define us. And so, they are never to be compromised.

In the words of the song:

मझधार में नैया डोले तो मांझी पार लगाए,

मांझी जो नाव डुबोये, उसे कौन बचाए

What is the solution?

In my view the solution is very simple. Justice. Let justice be done. Murder is a crime. It is fashionable today to call for tougher laws. The fact of the matter is that our existing law is more than sufficient. Murder is a crime and its punishment is death. What more can anyone do? The issue is not with the law but with the implementation of the law. When murder done by someone special is not punished, changing the law and making it tougher is not the solution. The solution is to bring the criminal to justice, by proper investigation of the crime and collection of evidence. It is not possible for any police force to anticipate a crime of random violence. Neither is it possible for the police to prevent such crimes from happening because we have no knowledge of hidden things. The only way to be forewarned about the possibility of such crimes is through Community Policing by building trust in civil society such that the Police Force is seen as their compatriot and friend. I know that there are a few officers who are working to this end. But one incident of extra-judicial killing destroys years of trust building.

It may not be possible to prevent every crime of politically motivated random violence but it is eminently possible to investigate a crime once it happens and catch the criminals. When there is a price that the criminal is convinced he will have to pay, then he will think many times before committing the crime. Instead of that, when innocent people are killed because the police is too lazy to investigate or is subservient to others and has accepted the role of hitman, then instead of fighting terrorism, you end up creating more terrorists. An extra-judicial killing is a dream come true for the terror group recruiter. Every real terrorist killed in a staged encounter gives birth to ten more recruits. Every innocent killed in a staged encounter gives birth to a hundred. The nightmare of the genuine law enforcer is the false encounter because it closes doors of cooperation which could have prevented future crimes.

My suggestion is that given the dismal record of police investigations, it is time for civil society to launch an independent investigation into these terror crimes and encounters. We need to set up a fund to pay for a top-class investigation agency to independently investigate the crime and collect evidence. This can then be given publicly to the police to take to a conclusion. I say publicly because if the police know that there is real evidence then trying to cover up is not so easy. Criminals must be punished and not rewarded, if we are serious about fighting crime. If crime pays, criminals will flourish. If criminals start paying, crime will end. The law must be respected and applied, no matter who tries to break it.

If we do that, then we would have taken the right steps to change the script. Once the script is changed, the results will be different. It is time for us to wake up and realize that polluting the water in the lake affects all those who live in the lake. Those who sit quietly will not escape the effects of pollution.

The time has come to speak and to act if we want to bequeath a world to our children that they will not curse us for. Stand for justice. Speak for justice. Or sit silently and support the terrorist, the murderer and the oppressor.

The choice is yours. I made mine a long time ago.

Fact is stranger than fiction

I discovered a new word: Mitron. It means, 'A large group of unsuspecting people about to be hit by something they will take a long time to recover from.' Ironically it comes from the Hindi word – Mitron (Mitr = friend. Mitron = of friends). I believe we are in a Mitron moment; the discovery of a word and an experiential understanding of its true meaning.

Demonetization has hit us all but it hit the poor the most. People who live on the knife edge of society which can change overnight from a life of dignity to a life as a beggar on the street. People who have no 'nest egg', no safety net, no backup. I recall two things as I write this article. One is an article by my good friend, Prof. Madhukar Shukla of XLRI who wrote about these people on the knife edge; the other is one of my own very early consulting assignments. Let me tell you about that.

In the late 80's I was hired by The Commonwealth Trust to assess a very interesting economic development program that they had initiated in East Delhi (how many Delhiites even know that East Delhi exists?). The program was well-intentioned in that it offered interest-free loans to 'small entrepreneurs' but with the condition (supposed to be a benefit) that they pair up with corporate executives so that they could teach them a thing or two about business. My first thought, as an IIMA grad was, 'I can smell an MBA behind this from a mile away'. I say that because it was a theoretically sound approach without due thought given to reality on the ground. Let me explain.

The loans given were to 'small entrepreneurs'. I keep using apostrophes for this term to underline what 'small' meant.

Rs. 3000 (which wasn't all that much even in the 80's) was the average loan amount. It was given to the Istri-wala (mobile clothes iron man).

This wonderful picture will bring to mind the man (most cases it is his wife who works on this cart) whose services every one of us urban Indians have benefited from. We send down clothes to him from our fancy apartments as he parks his push-cart in the street outside our compound wall. He irons our shirts and trousers, sarees and skirts, charges a few rupees which we pay in **cash** and he moves on to the next building or villa. What he earns that day pays for the rent of his 'house' (this article is getting too full of apostrophes), school fee for his children (you can't keep people from aspiring), and food for his family. That money is what keeps him on the knife edge and saves him from falling off and coming to your house with a begging bowl in hand. The Commonwealth Trust offered small loans to people like him, the vegetable vendor, the cobbler, the shoeshine guy, the bicycle repairer, the truck tire puncture repairman and similar 'small entrepreneurs'. The biggest loan had been given to a man who had a printing press with a single machine in a small shop where you had to turn sideways to get past the machine.

As I mentioned, the 'fringe benefit' according to the initiator of the scheme and The Commonwealth Trust was the partnership between this small entrepreneur and a corporate executive. The corporate executive with his education and presumably greater understanding was supposed to help the small entrepreneur to keep good accounts, pay tax, use technology, build a customer base, survey his market and make growth plans. The formal introductory meeting was arranged in a five star hotel with tea and samosa in an atmosphere of pretended equality between partners and the pairs were made. Three years later, the project came up for evaluation and that is where I came in.

That is also when I discovered East Delhi and that too in July. Those who have lived in Delhi in summer without air conditioning may understand what I went through. The lanes of the area of East Delhi are so narrow that even a Maruti 800 can't drive through them. I would leave my hired car on the main road and either walk or take a local auto rickshaw. I preferred the latter because the driver knew the people who I wanted to meet and usually told me stories about them later after being a silent listener to the conversation that I had with them. I spent two weeks on this assignment and learned what every Tandoori Chicken knows—what the inside of a tandoor feels like. East Delhi was also one of the places most affected by the anti-Sikh pogrom of 1984, the perpetrators of which still walk free while the victims suffer in silence. But then in a country where to break the law with impunity is a status symbol, that's understandable and expected.

To return to my story, I met these small entrepreneurs, every single one of them. I sat with them in (or near) their businesses. I drank tea with them (which bless our culture, our poor are those who uphold it) which they insisted on paying for and asked them how their business was going and how their partnership was doing. All conversations were in Hindi but I am translating here for your benefit.

Me: Namashkar Jee, how are you. I am Yawar Baig and have come from The Commonwealth Trust to ask you a few questions about your business.

He: Namashkar Sahib. I am repaying my loan on time. I have not defaulted.

Me: (as red in the face as someone with my complexion can get): No, no, no! I didn't come to ask about repayment. Of course, you are repaying on time. You have a great record. The Commonwealth Trust is very pleased about this. I have only come to ask how things are going with you and with the partnership that was made with Mr. So-and-so.

He: (relieved smile followed by shifting eyes): All is well Sahib.

Me: Please don't call me Sahib. My name is Yawar.

He: Jee Achcha Yawar Sahib. (I gave up after trying for some time).

Me: So how is it going? Do you meet each other? How often do you meet?

He: (eyes shifting again): All is well Yawar Sahib.

Me: (persevering): Do you meet each other? How often do you meet?

He: (realizing that I won't go away): Sahib, we have not met after that first meeting.

Me: (genuinely shocked): Why? Why didn't you meet? What happened?

He: (hurriedly): Sahib, it is not his fault. You see I tried to meet him several times. But Sahib, I am a small man (hum chotay aadmi hain. Wo baday aadmi hai). He is a big man. I went to his Kothi (mansion – Hindi for big house – not necessarily a mansion but he calls it Kothi to honor its owner). But his Chowkidaar (security guard) turned me away. He refused to believe me that Sahib had asked me to come. Yawar Sahib, I am a small man but I have izzat (honor, dignity). I didn't go there to ask for charity. I went there because they said that we were partners and I could talk to him any time. But if the Chowkidaar turns me away, I won't go again and again.

Me: (at a loss for words): But didn't he give you his phone number? Couldn't you call him and tell him to speak to his Chowkidaar?

He: I did Yawar Sahib. He told me to meet him in his office. But there it was worse. So, I gave up.

Me: But this partnership was supposed to help you. What did you do when you couldn't even meet your partner?

He: Yawar Sahib, the truth is, how can he help me when he knows nothing of my reality. He lives in a different world from mine. So, different that he can't even imagine what my world is like. I agreed to the partnership because that was a condition of getting the loan. I never expected that it would work. And it didn't. I am most grateful to The Commonwealth Trust for the loan. I needed that. The partnership I didn't need, so it doesn't matter.

Me: (wondering what I am going to write in my report): What did you do when you needed any advice?

He: I went to my Mamaji (uncle or father in law) and sometimes to my neighbor (essentially his competitor) and asked them. They advised me and I followed their advice.

Me: Your competitor gave you advice about your business which was good for you? Isn't he your competitor?

He: (shocked at my ignorance): Of course, he gave me good advice. He is my competitor but first he is my brother (from my community, extended family etc). Of course, he gave me good advice. He is easy to reach. We have a relationship, a real relationship, not only business and above all, he understands my reality because he is a part of it.

This conversation was more or less what I had with every one of those in that survey. One common factor with all of them was that their entire business was in cash. After all, when was the last time you paid the Istri-wala or the Sabji-wala or the Bai who comes to clean your home and cook your meal and the many walas our life quality depends on, by cheque or credit card? All their business is in cash and so is the business of all those in the value chain they deal in; those they buy the necessities of their lives from. All cash. Out of their meagre and harsh existence it is the genius Indian woman that they save some money – again cash. They don't bank it. They buy gold if they can or just keep the cash. It is their saving for an emergency and since the biggest requirement of emergencies is liquidity, they like cash. Sometimes this saving is done over such a long period that it amounts to a good bit; maybe three to five lakhs (3-500, 000). But that is what they slogged and sweated for over decades. Should that be taxed? Especially in a country that has no social security, no emergency services to speak of and no support for such people except what they can get from their savings and families.

Indeed, they don't declare this income to the Government. They don't bank it because every trip to the bank means a loss of business. They need cash and in cash they trust. It is not for nothing that even in bigger establishments you may have seen the sign, 'IN GOD WE TRUST. REST STRICTLY CASH.' That is not a statement of religiosity but of hard reality. Does that make them 'black marketeers' and thieves? Sure, these small businessmen and women don't pay tax but they contribute to the economy both directly by buying and indirectly by providing services. They add value and quality to our lives and take away the drudgery of daily chores. It is all these people who are the true backbone of the economy. It is they who spread goodness all around them because of the food chain that they are part of and support. It is they who create neighborhoods which are dynamic and alive though overall poor. Unlike dead American inner cities which are home to the poor in Western societies. And these, our poor, our small entrepreneurs, our salt of the earth man and woman who are the hardest hit in this Mitron moment of demonetization.

I was reminded of all this when I read this interview:

http://scroll.in/article/823231/interview-demonetisation-has-hit-80-of-small-businesses-the-sector-is-staring-at-apocalypse

I was reminded about this because the demonetization move has once again underlined the fact about our society that decisions that affect millions are taken by those who are as foreign to them as Martians would be to us Earthlings. People who either don't understand their reality or couldn't care less. People who don't even think of them as a 'vote bank', because momentarily, votes can be bought or swayed by tearful oratory. And that is enough to get elected and then it doesn't matter what those who voted think or feel; survive or perish. People, who even if they knew that reality once upon a time, have chosen to forget it and take pride in associating with the high and mighty rather than with those who they were born among and grew up with. But then you can't fault a person for his aspirations, can you? As long as rhetotrick (my coinage – it means tricky rhetoric) is in plentiful supply, facts don't matter. What happened doesn't matter as long as its creators can give it a positive spin. Human life is not cheap. It is priceless. Has no price. Is free. (not the usual inference of the word, 'priceless', I realise).

One economist friend said to me, "The economy will take a decade to recover from this move." I said to him, 'Economies don't 'recover' in a decade. They are replaced because all those who participated in the old economy have perished.' 'Recover' is a term that economists use on their neat charts. The reality is neither neat nor painless. India's economy 'recovered' after the Bengal Famine. But 2 million people perished. Economists don't care about that. Not that they are heartless. It is just that they don't have the language to express the monetary value of sweat and tears, of life and death. Numbers are used so much because they are neat and help us to remain out of touch with reality. When our reality, that which we have jointly created, is so painful, nasty and brutal, we need tools to keep it at bay. Numbers are one. Entertainment is another. We need to forget reality. The alternative is to change reality so that we don't need to forget it, can enjoy it and benefit from it. But that takes too much trouble. It is easier to forget.

I mention this here because in this race to garner all resources for oneself without a thought about others, we have created a society that is crying out in pain and grief. It is inconceivable to imagine that the resources of the world can possibly be concentrated in the hands of so few, but as they say, 'fact is stranger than fiction'. I can imagine the derision or at best amused smiles if any author dared to suggest that 62 people would own 50% of global assets and the rest of the world would watch silently. But that is not fiction. That is fact.

https://www.theguardian.com/business/2016/jan/18/richest-62-billionaires-wealthy-half-world-population-combined

For perspective, let me state that a bus has 65 seats excluding the driver's seat.

Anesthetized Anarcy

We, in India, are living in a state of anesthetized anarchy.

We seem to have lost it in more ways than one. In the days of the sabretooth tiger, mankind needed to be totally in touch with reality if it wished to avoid being the tiger's next meal. Since we made the STT extinct we seem to believe that being in touch with reality is not required or at least, is optional. The fact is, that it is neither optional nor unnecessary. It is as critical now as it was then, with the only difference that the one who eats you now has changed; you are still on the menu!

As I read what members of the present Bhakti movement are writing with respect to present conditions in India and what the wise gurus of corporate fame speak from their elevated platforms, I pinch myself to remember that the laws that run the world are not made by them and that the One who made those laws hasn't changed them yet.

Nandan Nilekanni at the TiE Convention, for example, takes his constitutional on stage and while he exercises walking back and forth, forcing you to do some neck yoga, he tells you how the volume of electronic monetary transactions has gone up from the time people used to send money orders and how in the last three years more people transferred money electronically than they did via money orders for the past one hundred years. That, he declares to a rapt TiE audience, is a sign of development. Audience claps. Behold, anesthetized anarchy in action.

What he forgets to say, and those feverishly forwarding the video of this wonderful speech forget to ask, is what percentage of population that volume of monetary transaction represents. What is the reality? The reality is that the total percentage that does electronic banking is 2% of the population of India. So, whatever you want to say about how monetary volumes have increased, they are still all within that 2%. What, therefore, is the real meaning of the numbers being marketed?

The problem of geeky thinking is nicely mentioned in this article as the 'empathy vacuum', the bane of life of those who are used to binary thinking and playing with imaginary numbers until they begin to believe in their own creations. What is starkly visible in our country today is a total absence of empathy for those whose lives have been wrecked by the demonetization drive.

Secondly, comparing historical data about the health of an economy using monetary transactional volume alone doesn't take into account the value of money itself. A person in 1900 sent Rs. 10 by money order. The same person, if he lived that long, in 2000 would have to send Rs. 100,000 by electronic transfer to cover the same expense. So, how does the higher number indicate greater prosperity? But it seems that we have pickled our brains. Statistics can be made to say whatever you want them to say. And that is the game being played. The reason that game succeeds is because we don't think and don't ask questions.

Behold, anesthetized anarchy in action.

I call it anesthetized because we are the only country in the world where dozens of people can simply die standing in a line to withdraw money from the bank because of the liquidity crunch that the government imposed, but nothing happens.

We're the only country perhaps in the history of the world where money is demonetized in a thriving economy. As someone said, 'That is like shooting the tires of a racing car in a race', but nothing happens. We're the only country in the world which pays no attention to the opinions of Nobel Prize winning scholars, financial experts and bankers and instead applauds politicians whose understanding of economics is exemplified in the measures that have led, which has forced the rest of to take an interest in economics. Instead of protests, people say that this is the price we (not them, mind you) must pay for 'cleaning' the economy http://bit.ly/2gJhsWa

So, what is our reality?

1. We are World No. 1 in absolute poverty far ahead of sub-Saharan Africa.
2. We are World No. 1 in farmer suicides. (is there a global standard for this?)
3. We are World No. 1 in human trafficking. Add bonded labor and we will be World No. 1 in slavery.
4. We are close to the top in illiteracy.

5. Our unemployment figures are mind boggling and just went up thanks to this new initiative to make India cashless. Amazing how quickly that target was achieved.

6. 80% of our graduates are unemployable which tells you something about the quality of our education.

7. Corruption is not only acceptable at all levels of society but it is aspirational.

8. Our politicians and executives (civil service) are mostly corrupt and judiciary is trying to catch up.

9. We have zero tolerance, not for corruption and lies, but for those who dare to speak out against it.

10. Our view of religion is not something that binds people and joins hearts together but something that divides and must be brutally enforced.

11. We have confused loyalty to a political party for loyalty to the country and have branded all dissent anti-national and unpatriotic.

12. We elect politicians to office only if they belong to our caste, irrespective of everything else.

13. That our politicians are corrupt, mostly uneducated and many have criminal records (including murder), matters not at all in our reckoning. We still elect them.

14. Human life doesn't have low value in our country; it has no value at all. From 2005 to 2015, over 300,000 farmers committed suicide in India. Result? http://bit.ly/1Lisiy3

15. To break the law with impunity is a measure of social status and an accepted status symbol and is treated as a matter of right by the high and mighty. All of them invariably get away with this, thus reinforcing the principle that some people are more equal than others.

16. Undertrial prisoners are routinely killed by police and the killers are applauded by the media and titled, 'Encounter Specialist'.

17. Our rape, murder and plunder statistics would do credit to a war zone.

18. In terms of productivity, quality and industry we can't even compare ourselves to Bangladesh, but we feel free to compare ourselves to China. http://bit.ly/2gjOHTa

That is why I call it anesthetized because despite all this, our Bhakti Movement is going strong. Thank god for our blind supporters. People are telling tales to one another voluntarily, blind-folded to the reality imagining that if they tell the tale long enough and shout down any dissent, their tale will come true. This is because those of us who live in cities and are in the so-called upper middle class and grace the stage of entertainment shows like Times Now and others, live in echo chambers. We shout out our opinions and then count the echoes as agreement. All our projections are based on the number of times we heard our own voice echo back to us bouncing off the walls of our echo chambers. We make the most noise. We are the most visible and others like us assess the state of India based on this.

But anyone who has travelled in rural India, where the vast majority of our people live, will tell you a very different tale. A tale of deprivation, crops left to rot in the field or fed to goats because there is no cash to harvest them. The woman who has one buffalo whose milk she sells to her neighbors will tell you that neighbors won't pay for that milk by credit card. Buffaloes with credit card slots have yet to be born. That woman needs the money in cash that very day to buy food to eat and feed her family. If the money is paid to her bank account on the basis of monthly credit (this is the solution that our accountant friends will instantly give you because they don't know one end of a buffalo from the other) she won't have money to eat today and tomorrow. And long before the first month's amount comes in, she and her buffalo will both have become history.

The Indian farmer, the man who sells bananas on a push cart, the fish seller who buys fish from the fisherman and sells it in the market, the daily wage earner on a construction site who works through a searing summer for ten hours to earn Rs. 200 with which to feed his family, will all tell you similar stories. For them 'cashless' means only one thing — that which they are suffering today. The demonetization initiative, no matter how noble its intentions, has converted these poor people into 'criminals' because they don't have bank accounts and don't pay tax so their earning is labelled 'black money'. Demonetization has become demonization and has converted them and us into beggars, unable to withdraw our own hard-earned savings on which we paid tax, from our own bank accounts. That this violates our Constitutional Right to property is one of those things that we dare not speak of for fear of being branded anti-national, seditious and god-knows what else. So, we don't protest. We applaud the noble initiative and thank god that the dead farmer, fisherman, milk seller, buffalo or random individual who dropped dead in a bank queue was not our mother, sister, brother, son, father, spouse. One must always be grateful.

Economies are not electric lights to be switched on and off at will. Especially not an economy as fragile and complex as the Indian economy. The effect of lost crops will not reverse until the next season. People's lost faith in the currency and in the entire banking system will not change to trust overnight. What this will do to liquidity needs no imagination to visualize. People's sudden fear of being literally cashless that has led to postponing purchasing decisions will not increase money supply. Nor will that fear suddenly be replaced by confidence. Our spending has slowed or stopped, our charity has slowed or stopped, our entertaining, holidays, all discretionary spending has slowed or stopped. All these things are the lifeblood of the nation. Where will the transfusion that we need come from?

Firmans are easy to issue but their effects are not in the control of the issuer. Neither can those effects be stopped or reversed by a counter Firman. Just as you can't order clouds to rain, you can't order crops to grow or the dead to come back to life. The laws of the world don't change. The one who chooses to shut his eyes to the signs of the sabretooth tiger will surely be his next meal. So, dream on.

Money, Money, Money

Dire Straits' famous song has some very politically incorrect lyrics but the refrain, 'Money for nothing and the chicks for free' sums up the situation of black marketeers and owners before the demonetization and the name of the songsters – Dire Straits – sums up their situation in India today. But what are the implications of demonetization? We have seen many theories, conspiracy and otherwise. One of the best articles that I have read is by former Finance and Economic Affairs Secretary, Arvind Mayaram, which is here:

http://www.asianage.com/opinion/interview-of-the-week/131116/economy-takes-a-hit-if-faith-in-the-paper-we-called-currency-is-shaken-arvind-mayaram.html

Let's see what the real, on-the-street effects of demonetization are and what their implications can be.

Effects:

We are a cash economy and that is not because we have a huge number of people with black money, but because we have a huge number of poor people who don't have bank accounts and don't deal with anything other than cash. For anyone who has lived or travelled in rural India this needs no explaining. So, I will not waste your time trying to describe what we have seen and experienced all our lives in our country without any problem or complaint. Those who need convincing can try to buy vegetables, fish, eggs, meat or chicken and pay for them with a credit card or cheque. Both buyers and sellers are not evil hoarders and black marketeers but ordinary, garden variety men and women trying to live their lives. This money that is earned by the sellers in never enough to be deposited in a bank. It is used to buy food and necessities for their families, goods to sell the next day and a little bit to set aside for a rainy day. This may accumulate over the years to some thousands. Do these people have documentary evidence about where they got this money from? Can they show that they paid tax on it? Can they show accounts of what they earn daily? Does the vegetable seller, the meat, fish or egg seller have a P&L account and a Balance Sheet? Does she have a PAN card? Does that therefore make them criminals?

Another situation is that of the middle-class housewife. Her husband gives her money to run the home, every month. She may only have completed primary school (in many cases she may not even be literate) but is a master economist. She manages to run a very good home, cook great meals, ensure that everyone has what they need and still she is able to save some money which she keeps hidden in the house. She doesn't have a bank account. She doesn't even want a bank account because it involves documentation that she can't manage on her own and if she asks anyone in the family to help, her secret will be revealed. She doesn't tell her husband or anyone about this but some day when one of her family needs something urgently she digs into her stock and surprises everyone by saving their skins. Is she a criminal because she does all this secretly? She is not an evil schemer. She is my and your mother.

Now comes demonetization and whatever it did to the illegal funds of political parties and black-market wizards, it also wiped out the savings of these people. That is what I am trying to interpret and find the bright side of.

The demonetization did wipe out the value of cash sitting in warehouses and suitcases of political parties and businessmen. And it did and will bring in cash into the vaults of banks who seem to have emptied those vaults lending to the same (or similar) businessmen who reneged on those loans. Those loans are still outstanding, post demonetization. The one who didn't repay the loan continues to enjoy his ill-gotten gains. But the middle class and poor of the country paid the bank on his behalf. That is a very neat arrangement, if you ask me.

How and why does black money get generated? The main driver is the fact that political parties are not compelled to show their sources of funds. This is the strangest of phenomena in a country where every individual is compelled to show where he earned his money from and must pay tax on it. Even charities in this country must apply for and get tax exemption failing which they have to pay tax on donations which they collect and disburse in charity. But a political party which gets a million times more, need not show how it got that money or from whom. I am sure I don't need to explain the implications of that on the black-market economy, corruption and hoarding. That situation remains as it is. So though the funds of those political parties and politicians who were not in the know reverted to their original value or less (Rs. 1000 = Rs. 5; in this case Rs. 0) the doors to accumulate such funds once again, no questions asked, remain open. As for those in the know, the originators of this idea, their associates, families and friends, mint employees and managers, drivers, secretaries, servants and others of power brokers and of course the usual suspects (friends in need), all had ample time to save their hoards.

As for all the talk about reducing fiscal expense and so on, Arvind Mayaram has spoken about that in the article above, so I won't repeat it. It must be obvious to anyone who knows what the word 'fiscal' means. What I want to repeat of what Arvind Mayaram said, which goes to the core of the issue in terms of the future, is the issue of faith. Not faith in god, but faith in paper.

People save money and keep those savings in paper currency because they believe that the value of their savings will not be nullified. They have faith in the currency though they know that the actual paper has no intrinsic value. Even though inflation erodes the value of their savings people don't convert their savings to gold or immovable property because liquidity is more important for them than whatever loss of value that may take place over time. This is what ensures that money remains in circulation and is not taken out of the market and parked in gold. Paper money exists because people have faith.

That is the reason also why in Islam, Zakat (@2.5%) is liable every year on gold and silver even if you have to sell some of the gold and silver to pay what you are liable to pay in that year. Obviously, this reduces your stock of gold and hypothetically speaking it can reduce over time to a level where you are no longer liable to pay Zakat. Despite that, Islam decreed that you must sell a part of the gold and give that money in charity because Islam recognized the importance of keeping money in circulation.

It doesn't take great imagination to see what will happen if people lose faith in the currency. That is the reason, as Mayaram says and we all know, the US dollar has never been demonetized though it is the most counterfeited currency and the most trusted currency in all black-market deals. Faith in the currency must be balanced against whatever negative effects that may happen because of unaccounted currency. Those negative effects must be neutralized in other ways, for example, by making political parties account for their cash inflows, state funding for elections and eliminating Income Tax.

Demonetizing currency destroys faith in the currency, discourages people from keeping their savings in paper money, encourages them to take their savings out of circulation because it pits importance of liquidity against saving the capital amount. It places huge hardship on the weakest and least influential people in society. It further disempowers those who are already the weakest; women (housewives, mothers), illiterate daily wage earners (headload workers, porters, construction workers, beggars), small business owners (you must understand this in the Indian context to know what I mean by 'small'), small service providers (rickshaw pullers, thela walas etc.).

It is easy for the powers that be to talk about accepting the inconvenience because they don't have to face it themselves and can easily turn a blind eye to the fact that a daily wage earner standing in a queue at a bank to exchange his life savings for the snazzy new currency is also losing his wage for that day. For many that is a very significant loss. For some it may mean that when they return the next day to their job, they find that the job has gone because someone else has been employed in their place. I won't list the kinds of suffering that housewives, the old and sick are undergoing standing for hours in serpentine queues. Those who are interested can go and talk to people standing in those queues. Or even better, go and stand in such a queue yourself to see how it feels to stand for six hours without food or water or shade or anywhere to rest your tired legs. People are doing more than that.

It is clear that the move to demonetize currency was taken without sufficient thought about all its intended and unintended consequences and without adequate preparation for its seamless and painless implementation. If that had been done, there would have been no reason for the tearful histrionics and theatrics that we are witnessing which are probably good for TRP ratings but not for anything else.

Whatever the effects of demonetization may prove to be on black money, what is clear is that faith in paper currency has taken a very big hit. I am not sure if this loss of faith can ever be restored. The thought that is uppermost in the minds of people is that if the government can do this once, it can do it again. And if one government can do it, then so can another government. Try to think of what conclusion the average man and woman standing in long queues to exchange old notes for new, who may even lose a part of his savings in this process, will come to.

Sadly, our media won't show us the truth as it is not viable for them. But ignoring the truth won't change it. Reality, unrecognized, has a nasty way of biting very hard when you are not looking. That is perhaps something that those who demonetized currency didn't think of. That is also something that may show its effect in the elections, the only place where politicians and political parties are held to account. Jai Hind.

Dhan Ki Baat

I read this article with great interest.

http://epaper.newindianexpress.com/c/21887818

The final sentence is salutary. I want to add that whether governments or judges guard or curtail rights will depend on what we, the people, do about it. Active citizenship is not something that we are used to. We are too used to being the 'ruled', looking up to our elected governments as (even calling them) 'rulers'. That they are not rulers is something that still remains to sink in, both in our consciousness and theirs. So they behave like feudal lords and we behave like serfs. We even have terms that stink of feudalism to this day, used by our administrators e.g. Collector's Peshi or Girijana Durbar.

That our elected leaders exist because we elected them will help us to understand our own responsibility for whatever is happening in the nation. Then we will change from being complainers to solution seekers. That is the real meaning of democracy, which I hope we will be able to embody.

Take the much mentioned 'demonetization'. I am not going to talk about its economic effects. Many more qualified than I have analyzed it threadbare and concluded that it was a body blow to the economy without a valid reason. All that our media has been able to say is that it will not affect BJP's chances of being elected again in 2019 because Modiji has changed his narrative. Little do they realize what that sounds like. Is election a matter of someone creating or promoting a story and the listeners reacting to it like rats to the pied piper's tune? But that is the result of living in two worlds, democracy in theory (in the mind) and feudalism in reality.

http://www.thecitizen.in/index.php/NewsDetail/index/1/11610/The-RBI-Report-And-The-Truth-About-Demonetization

What is far more significant in my view is the attitude and behavior around demonetization. It was a step taken in secrecy even from closest aides, all of whom expressed surprise before slipping their masks back on again. It was declared as a step taken by the Prime Minister on the advice of a man who is not a cabinet member or even in government. All to prevent owners of black money from escaping.

http://economictimes.indiatimes.com/news/politics-and-nation/here-is-the-man-who-advised-pm-modi-to-demonetise-rs-500-and-rs-1000-notes/articleshow/55339012.cms

We are told that the PM believed him and took this step almost unilaterally and issued a proclamation that from midnight of November 8, 2016. Kings issue proclamations. Not elected leaders. Elected leaders consult their council of ministers and in a matter as serious as this. They consult a larger cross section of leaders of the public (Opposition), perhaps even the public themselves. After all, the two excuses for demonetization; curbing black money and funding of terrorist activity' are laughably inaccurate, as subsequent events have shown beyond all doubt. That is why the narrative was changed to, 'We did it to make the country a cashless economy.'

Why would you change a narrative unless it had failed? After all, the earlier one of ridding the country of black money and terror funding and paying loads of money into the bank account of every Indian citizen sounded so much more exciting than saying that it was an exercise to support banks and credit card companies. Even more especially when the earlier statement was made so powerfully: http://www.abplive.in/india-news/demonetisation-even-if-you-burn-me-alive-i-am-not-scared-says-narendra-modi-445603 Burn me alive?? Drama sells.

So why change it? Incidentally, can I see a show of hands from all those who received cash in their accounts from the government as a result of return of black money including that secreted in Swiss Bank accounts? Political parties need not respond because after all the sweetest part of the change was that donations to political parties were sought to be exempted from disclosure. That is when I decided to start my own political party, Tan Man Dhan Mukti Morcha – TMDM² ©. All donations welcome.

http://indianexpress.com/article/india/india-others/political-parties-cant-be-under-rti-act-centre-tells-sc/

Well, India became cashless, but perhaps not in the way that the term 'cashless' is meant to be understood by the spin doctors.

To understand the 'cashlessness' of India, ask the housewife who saved small change from spending money that her husband used to give her, for thirty years and had Rs. 3 lakhs. Suddenly, on November 8, she was promoted to the status of a black marketer, money launderer (take your pick or invent your own names). Her legitimate savings, the symbol of our culture of family responsibility, caring for the future of others, the very spirit of motherhood, became illegitimate for her. On the face of it, all she had to do was to go to a bank and exchange it for the nice new colorful notes. But in reality, she would have had to open an account, get a PAN card, deposit the money, answer a million questions about where she got it from (all based on the assumption that she got them through illegitimate means) and pay tax on it. Tax on money which her husband had already paid tax on. And of course, she would have to answer to her husband (in many cases, a fate worse than death) about how she had all this money but never told him about it. That is how she entered the cashless economy by becoming cashless herself. As I mentioned, I am not talking GDP or economic numbers. I am talking about the izzat (honor, self-respect) of honest people, their feelings, family dynamics, domestic power equations and the disempowerment of ordinary people, especially women.

To understand the 'cashlessness' of India, ask those who died, standing in queues at banks. Of course, the dead tell no tales. India is perhaps the only country where something like this can happen, not once or twice but over one hundred times, unremarked. That nobody is called to account is not surprising when there is not even a demand that this should be done. I stand in line at the bank. Someone in the line before me, drops dead. They remove him. I move ahead one place and thank god for small mercies. What's remarkable? I am told that I am doing it for the nation. I am a vegetable, fish, eggs, or a banana seller, standing in line hoping that the bank will not give me a hard time asking me to open an account, PAN card and whatnot. I have enough to worry about. If someone dies in the line, well, what can I do?

To understand the 'cashlessness' of India, ask the people who had no notes to exchange because all their savings were in the bank already. But after November 8, when they wanted to withdraw some cash, they were told that they couldn't do so. Officially there was a limit to what they could withdraw. In reality, they couldn't withdraw anything at all as the bank had no currency notes to give out.

"How long will this last?"

"God knows", said the banker.

"How can you stop me from withdrawing my own money?"

"I am not stopping you. This is the instruction we have received."

"What can I do?"

"God knows", said the banker.

I go to the grocery store with my new colorful Rs. 2000 note. I need groceries worth Rs. 500.

"No!" said the grocery store owner, "You need groceries worth Rs. 2000; you just don't realize that."

"What do you mean?"

"I mean I don't have any change to give you. No notes. So, take your change in cabbages or eggs. Just keep and eat them."

"How long will this last?"

"God knows", said the grocer.

You see, this is why there's a shortage of atheists in India. You really do need to believe in God.

To understand the 'cashlessness' of India, ask those who till the land, labor from dawn to dusk on construction sites to feed their families, who sell food, provide services and add real value to people's lives. Ask the Istiriwala (mobile clothes ironing person), the Doodhwala (milk vendor), the Bayi (maid) who works in our homes, the Sabjiwala (vegetable seller), the Machiwala (fish seller). Not one of them had a bank account. Not one of them had a PAN card. Not one of them paid Income Tax. Every single one of them had a family to feed. Every single one of them had some savings put aside for a so-called 'rainy' day. Every single one of them suffered for no reason except that in our Feudal-Democracy (my coinage, please give credit if you use this term), it was proclaimed without warning that his savings were illegal until proven legal. He was guilty until proven innocent.

One good thing that happened because of this demonetization, which I am very pleased about. It was proven beyond all doubt that there is no corruption in India. After all, did you hear a single story of a policeman, income tax official, customs officer, bureaucrat or politician standing in a bank line trying to legitimize his bribe money? Did you hear of any of them dropping dead from exhaustion or guilt? So, what does it mean? It means that all that we always hear about corruption is nonsense. There is no corruption in India. Nobody takes bribes. All government officers and officials pay tax on all income, upar ki aur andar ki. Like elephant tusks and teeth, khanay kay alag, aur dikhanay kay alag. I will leave this untranslated in the spirit of the line of poetry:

> Tum samajh sako tho aansoo
> Na samajh sako tho pani

What is our, we the people's, reaction to all this? Silence or complaining. In public, we are silent. In private, we moan and groan, we blame and crib. In both places, we take no action. And when we are asked why, we reply, 'What can we do? We can do nothing.' This warrants another couplet:

> Kursi hai, tumhara yeh janaza tho nahin hai
> Kuch kar nahin saktay, tho utar kyon nahin jatay? ~ Irteza Nishat

This brings me back to the beginning of my argument which is that if we want good governance in a democracy, we have to participate in it. Serfs have no choice but to complain. Citizens are not serfs, no matter what their elected leaders (called 'rulers' in India) may like to think. Citizens must act like citizens and take an interest in governance.

Today we have a situation where the Ruling Party is doing what it considers best for the nation. You can hardly fault them on intention. We have an Opposition which sits silently by and watches while it claims to be against the policies of the Ruling Party. Why? The Opposition is muzzled because everyone is afraid of skeletons in their cupboards being exposed. But what is the solution? Because in the end it is we, the so-called common folk who are paying the price; we and our children. True, we are paying the price of electing corrupt leaders for decades, but that is not a luxury we can afford. Shortsightedness is not an asset when you are driving a car at 70 MPH. Ours is going faster than that. No change without pain. Pain is not something you opt for but accept to escape death. Think cancer treatment. What is happening is worse than that. Cancer only kills you. This will kill you and your future generations. So, what do you want to do? Yes, you and me.

For all change begins with the man in the mirror.

Normalizing Terror

We are free to choose but every choice has a price

"Hate: It has caused a lot of problems in this world, but it has not solved a single one yet." Maya Angelou

We seem to be living in times when some people appear to be bent on challenging this law of nature – that fire burns and the result is always ash.

The way people handle catastrophic news is as follows:
Shock > Grief > Anger > Hope > Faith

If, this cycle is interrupted, then a new ending happens. The new cycle becomes:
Shock > Grief > Anger > Hope > Despair

Beware the man who feels he has nothing to lose. Crime can be prevented. Crime must be prevented. As they say, 'prevention is better than cure'. In the case of crime this is even more important because like the case in point above, nothing that can be done now will ever restore the lives of those who were murdered for no reason other than they belonged to a particular religious group. I didn't put it like that because I am reluctant to use the word 'Muslim', but because Muslims are not the only ones at the receiving end. We had Sikhs killed in their hundreds (maybe thousands) when Indira Gandhi was assassinated and Congress was in power. They still await justice. We had churches burnt, priests and nuns killed, one burnt alive in his car with his two little children. They still await justice. We have Dalits who have been killed for decades and nobody even talks about justice for them. We had Muslims who were killed all over Gujarat in 2002 (one among hundreds of so-called riots all over India). We had two terms of Congress government rule thereafter, but the victims still await justice.

What I am trying to say is that what is happening in India today in the name of 'cow vigilantism' or extremism, is not new. Neither can the responsibility of it be laid at the door of the BJP alone. It is true that it is BJP in power today and so we look to them to ensure that justice is done and good governance is not sacrificed at the altar of political expediency. But that was and will always be our expectation from any government in power. Governments are supposed to govern. When they don't, the country loses. Not any individual or group, but the whole nation. Where the loss is likely to be irreplaceable, it is even more important to ensure that it doesn't happen in the first place.

This is why a strong system of crime investigation, community participation and swift justice plays a very powerful role in keeping the victims from the brink of despair. As long as people know that they have a viable alternative for redress of wrong, they will take that option every single time. But when they begin to see from experience after experience, that criminals always get away, crimes go unpunished, there is no hope for justice, compensation or retribution, then they fall into despair. Take the latest breaking news about the killers of Pehlu Khan, the dairy farmer who was slaughtered while he was legally, legitimately and justifiably transporting cows to his dairy farm.

http://indianexpress.com/article/india/alwar-lynching-gau-rakshaks-cow-vigilance-clean-chit-to-all-six-accused-named-by-pehlu-khan-in-dying-declaration-4843051/

I have no comments to make as I didn't handle the investigation. All I can say is that Pehlu Khan didn't commit suicide or drop dead on his own. He was killed. Before he died, he recognized and named his killers. So, if they are not guilty, who is? That is what the police and the State are supposed to find out and bring to book.

If Pehlu Khan's case was a Pehli-bar, then one wouldn't be as concerned. But this is like a broken record, or a bad penny (choose your own proverb), it seems to happen every time. Incident after incident, all with the same ending, nobody is guilty of the crime. Today there is a lot of justifiable concern to prevent radicalization of youth. What is needed is a frank assessment of what leads to radicalization and acceptance of the fact that it is lack of law enforcement and swift justice that leads to people falling into despair. That is a downward spiral that has only one end.

India is a land of contradictions. The only constant is diversity which we tolerate only by force. However, we are very comfortable living with complete contradictions as we live in compartments in our minds. Let me give you some examples: In India, we worship the woman – as a goddess – of everything from wealth to fertility to knowledge to music to power. But have no problems demanding dowry from the bride for the favor of marrying her and then burning her alive (or murdering her in other ways) if the dowry is not enough or if we simply decide later that we want more. Incidentally this is an Indian issue, not a Hindu one. Muslims for whom taking dowry is Haraam, do so under different pretexts, trying to deceive God and man. But they deceive nobody except themselves.

Of late, rape has become a national pastime with our august politicians saying in effect, 'Boys will be boys. Girls must not provoke them by dressing immodestly.' Another said, 'It is the effect of eating a lot of noodles.' He was from Haryana where apparently, they eat a lot of noodles. Muslims like to proclaim loudly for all those who care to listen that Islam treats women and men equally and gives rights to women that they don't have in many modern countries to this day. But they remain silent on the fact that Islam gives women these rights but Muslim men don't. So, Muslim women continue to be deprived of what their religion guarantees them.

Take food, which today has literally become a matter of life and death in our country. Beef is the main course in Kerala, Goa, Nagaland, Manipur, Assam, Arunachal Pradesh, Mizoram, Meghalaya (all Hindu majority states) and prohibited, banned, proscribed, Haraam in Kashmir (Muslim dominated state). But in UP, MP, Maharashtra, Rajasthan, Gujarat, if you say the word 'beef' without due respect, as determined by the Gau Rakshak (Cow Protector) who hears you, you will be summarily slaughtered without any problem or inconvenience to the slaughterers. Never mind that nobody in their right minds slaughters milk cows or buffaloes. It is bulls, male calves, or old cows which have run dry and are past yielding age which are slaughtered. That is an economic need of the farmer who can't afford to keep and feed them, so he sells them. Anyway, none of these logical arguments makes any sense. Nor does the fact that despite the fact that Gau Rakshaks rule the roost, India continues to be the largest exporter of beef to the world. How that is possible in a country where even if you talk about killing a cow, you will pay for that with your life, is, like the Indian Rope Trick and the Water of Ganges magician's tricks, an enduring mystery.

We worship snakes but slaughter the first one we see. We talk about Vasudev Kudumbakam (whole world is one family) but protect, uphold and propagate the caste system. We visit Lord Aiyappa on his hilltop residence, but we must first, by his order, pay respects to his Muslim friend, Vavar Swamy (resemblance to my name is accidental), whose temple (why a temple to a Muslim?) is at the foot of the hill. Millions do it, but it is Open Season on Muslims all over.

I can go on endlessly, but I won't. Why is this important? Because it shows up in attitudes in the workplace, society and politics. The ability to hold two opposing ideas simultaneously in the mind is a sign of intelligence. The ability to hold two opposing values simultaneously in the heart is a sign of hypocrisy. In this we are very skilled and entirely at ease.

The question is, where will this lead us? It is a rhetorical question to which I am sure we all know the answer.

Terror is fire.
Fire always burns.
And the result is always ash.

"Our lives begin to end the day we become silent about
things that matter."
Martin Luther King, Jr.

Now What?

Gauri Lankesh was executed. What else do you call a bullet in the forehead? We know why. The question to those who did it and those who supported it is, 'Now what?'

https://www.nytimes.com/2017/09/06/world/asia/gauri-lankesh-india-dead.html?mcubz=0

The problem with using 'ultimate' strategies is that when they fail, you have nothing left. Ultimate strategies also indicate another fatal flaw, that you are desperate. Nothing is working. So, you try the last weapon in your arsenal, the most powerful which came with a warranty to destroy all in its path. You fire it. You wait. The explosion fades. The smoke blows away. The dust settles. But just as you are about to heave a sigh of relief, you hear a voice, then another, then another; just like the one you tried to silence. And you stand there, smoking gun in hand, empty magazine, wondering, 'Now what?'

Hegel said, "We learn from history that we do not learn from history." If only we read and try to learn from history. But then those who killed Gauri and those who are engaged in manufacturing fake news or earning their living as internet trolls can hardly be blamed for not reading.

History is replete with incidents of attempts to muzzle the voices of truth and justice. Anyone who reads history can only come to one simple conclusion, that ideas must be responded to by ideas. Arguments must be met with counter arguments based on facts and logic. Not by shouting, screaming, accusations, threats or bullets. But as I quoted Hegel, 'We learn from history that we do not learn from history.' That is why another quote which is attributed to so many people that I place it before you, crediting all those who may have said it, 'Nations that don't learn from history are condemned to repeat it.'

The purpose of all such attempts at intimidation, be it the tirade against Hamid Ansari or Amir Khan or the final step of the murder of Gauri Lankesh, is to create such an atmosphere of fear that people will censor themselves. Make such an example of those who refuse to be intimidated that the rest of them will learn a lesson. What those who propound that theory fail to ask is the final question, 'What lesson will they learn?'

Take the situation today in this country. We had a nation which was quoted in the world in terms of its economic growth and its glowing future. Admittedly, we had our flaws—don't we all? But we could stand in the middle of the chowraha (traffic intersection) and criticize the government without any fear of reprisal. Our Prime Minister was a scholar in his own right, an economist, a teacher and a man respected worldwide. Yet we could call him Maun Mohan Singh referring to his famous refusal to speak on different occasions without the fear of his devotees jumping down our throats. Freedom was the key word in our country, including the freedom to urinate in public, but that is another matter. Today that is the only freedom that seems to have remained if I am to go by a video that someone sent me of someone relieving himself in the Delhi Metro. https://www.youtube.com/watch?v=m244-kV_h8A

We now have a situation where a young boy is murdered in a train filled by people including police officers and when the crime is sought to be investigated, there are no witnesses.

http://www.hindustantimes.com/delhi-news/how-could-they-hate-us-so-much-family-in-shock-after-16-year-old-muslim-boy-stabbed-to-death-on-train/story-TEzAfE9atfWvoEHaXJm6JJ.html

We have the father of an Air Force Officer, murdered on suspicion that he had beef in his fridge. We have a man slaughtered in broad daylight for transporting a cow for his dairy business when he had all the relevant permissions to do so. We even have officials of one state (Tamilnadu), officially deputed to transport cattle, assaulted and injured for doing their duty. We have a young man in Pune, lynched because he was wearing a cap. The instances of public lynching by what are called Cow Vigilantes are so many now that listing them is not possible here. The instances of online intimidation and abuse are myriad and instantaneous. What is remarkable and should be remarked on is not the incidents but the fact that they all go unpunished. No government can prevent crime totally. But any government worth the name must investigate it and bring the culprits to book. That is what a government is for. It is for governing. Not to dictate what people must eat, how they must dress, what they must and must not speak, who or what they should worship, but to govern the country in a way that keeps citizens safe. The government is not responsible for the incident but for what happens or fails to happen thereafter. That is what a government exists for. When crime goes unpunished, it spawns more crime. But of course, if the definition of crime is changed, then a crime is no longer a crime and the government is free from blame.

Safety and terror are both buzzwords today which are guaranteed to get attention. The problem is that today safety seems to be guaranteed for those who spread terror. While those who are being terrorized are not even allowed the freedom to mention it even mildly. Ask Hamid Ansari.

Will the murderers of Gauri Lankesh be apprehended and hanged? Will the murderers of Akhlaaq, Hafiz Junaid, Mohsin Sadiq Shaikh and dozens of others be similarly brought to book? Will I stop asking stupid questions?

When this government came to power in 2014, it did so on the promise of economic development. As the country with the largest number of people in abject poverty in the world, it is economic development that we need like a blood transfusion. That is why we elected this government. But what did we get instead?

Demonetization, which destroyed thousands of livelihoods, impoverished those living on the brink, sank SME's which are the backbone of society, wiped out the savings of the poor and did nothing to the black money and terror funding that it allegedly was aimed at. Anyone who knows anything about economics could have predicted this and many did. But this 'surgical strike' (not my coinage) on the economy was done with such swiftness that predictions had no meaning. Then came the implementation of GST. Another body blow to the economy that took down those left standing after demonetization. An initiative with noble intentions but the way it was done was to create confusion and despair, albeit giving rise to a completely new multi-crore business of GST Advisors.

What we were promised was development, Sab ka Saath Sab ka Vikas. What we got instead was apartheid, oppression and for those who dared to raise their voice, intimidation and murder. What we were promised was Ache Din. What we are now promised is New India. What we were promised was elimination of black money, bringing back money from Swiss bank accounts and depositing money into the accounts of all Indians. What we are now promised is Cashless India. What we were promised was development for all Indians. What we are now promised is....

Well, as Hegel said, "We learn from history that we do not learn from history." My question to myself and you is, "Do you want to prove him right or wrong?"

Radicalisation

One of my friends sent me this article and asked for my opinion.

http://www.firstpost.com/india/we-are-losing-kashmir-to-islam-ten-ways-to-counter-radicalisation-in-india-2997302.html

My answer: Actually what this guy proposes is quite tame. See what some others did:

Albania: the only European country with a majority Muslim population was ruled by Enver Halil Hoxha (born Muslim), communist leader of Albania from 1944 until his death in 1985. According to Hoxha, the surge in anti-religious activity began with the youth. The result of this "spontaneous, unprovoked movement" was the closing of all 2,169 churches and mosques in Albania. State atheism became official policy, and Albania was declared the world's first atheist state. Religiously based town and city names were changed, as well as personal names. During this period, religiously based names were also made illegal. The Dictionary of People's Names, published in 1982, contained 3,000 approved, secular names. In 1992, Monsignor Dias, the Papal Nuncio for Albania appointed by Pope John Paul II, said that of the three hundred Catholic priests present in

Albania prior to the Communists coming to power, only thirty survived. The number of Muslim Imams, Ulama who simply vanished, is not even known. All Madrassas were shut down. All religious practices and all clergymen (Imams, Khateebs, Ulama) were outlawed and those religious figures who refused to give up their positions were either arrested or forced into hiding.

The Party focused on atheist education in schools. During holy periods such as Lent and Ramadan many forbidden foods (dairy products, meat, etc.) were distributed in schools and factories, and people who refused to eat those foods were denounced. Starting on 6 February 1967, the Party began a new offensive against religion. Hoxha, who had declared a "Cultural and Ideological Revolution" after being partly inspired by China's Cultural Revolution, encouraged communist students and workers to use more forceful tactics to promote atheism, including violence. Sound familiar, Indians?

In 1985, Hoxha died after spending some time in a wheelchair. Albania today is still the poorest European country, but has a thriving religious life with both Christianity and Islam alive and well. Masaajid are full and Madrassas freely teach Islam. Hoxha and his period are cursed as a very dark and miserable period in Albanian history.

<u>**Soviet Union:**</u> Does anyone even remember the Soviet Union? USSR? The Russia of old? The Soviet Union was a state comprising fifteen communist republics which existed from 1922 until its dissolution into a series of separate nation states in 1991. Of these fifteen republics, six had a Muslim majority—Azerbaijan, Kazakhstan, Kirghizia, Tajikistan, Turkmenistan, and Uzbekistan. There was also a large Muslim presence in the Volga-Ural region and most of the population of North Caucasus of the Russian Federation were Muslims. A large number of Tatar Muslims lived in Siberia and other regions.

The Soviets tried every trick in the book, including purges (uncounted millions died in the Gulags of Siberia for no fault other than that they worshipped Allah ﷻ), forcibly removing children from their homes to study in atheist boarding schools. Masaajid were shut down, all public display of Islam was forbidden and brutally punished, youth were banned from praying in congregation in the Masaajid and anyone who disobeyed, vanished. This happened at different levels of intensity from 1922 – 1991.

The result: https://www.rt.com/news/316327-moscow-mosque-largest-europe/ President Vladimir Putin inaugurated a new mosque in Moscow which is supposed to be the largest mosque in Europe. Thousands of Russian

Muslims attended the ceremony. And half a million people pray Eid Salah in Moscow alone

https://www.youtube.com/watch?v=DL9HNU4U_Ak

And there are other examples including Communist China to this day and France and the unofficial oppression of Muslims in Europe and America. Going further back in history gives us even more graphic examples of the attempts to wipe Islam off the face of the earth. Genghis Khan slaughtered one million Muslims in one day in Samarkhand. And his grandson Hulegu laid Baghdad waste, killing every man, woman and child. America in Iraq has been busy exceeding these numbers from the 1990's onwards. Result? The Mongols and Tartars became Muslim and became the backbone of Islam all through Soviet Russia's attempts to wipe out Islam. Those who tried to wipe out Islam became its greatest supporters and defenders. To this Allama Iqbal said, 'Paasbaan mil gaye Kabay ko sanam khanay say' (The Kaaba got supporters from the temple). Welcome to learn from history. Or welcome to try. Your call.

The fact remains that the earth still belongs to Allahﷻ. We will all still die. And we will return to Allahﷻ. This is a fundamental law like gravity. You ignore it only at your own peril.

Lesson?

Killing and oppression only makes the survivors stronger, more rigid, more ruthless and more difficult to find and kill. The blow that doesn't break your back only strengthens you. But the willfully ignorant like the author of the 'We're losing Kashmir to Islam' article continue blindfolded and their sponsors like to listen to their insane rants. Instead what would be very instructive is to read some history and use some intelligence – even if you have to borrow it.

We are losing Kashmir. That's true. But that has nothing to do with Islam and everything to do with the manipulative corrupt politics of Kashmir supported by the different Governments of India for seventy years. We're losing the millions who we dismiss as Naxals, who're also Indian, remember? And not Muslim. We're losing. That's because our policies are more and more skewed. We're also going to lose twenty crore (200 million) Muslims in the rest of India if we don't do something about justice.

Kashmir is a combination of bad politics and self-serving leaders from Day 1. And that's continued for seventy years. What we're seeing today is the cumulative effect. Like Pakistan, Kashmir is also ruled by three or four Ruling Families, all Muslim in name and nothing more. And every government including this one has colluded with them. What Kashmir needs is real democracy. Not this sham that comes through the barrel of a gun. Kick out the ruling families. Tell Kashmiris to decide their future and your problem is solved. But maybe that's been left too long already.

The reality is that the security forces are committing atrocities and have been doing that for decades. It's understandable that there may be instances of shooting in a situation like Kashmir because of the risk to the security forces and consequently heightened tension. But rape? What's the justification for rape? Nobody can deny that's not only happening but is very common. That's worse than death. And leaves wounds to the soul which can never be healed. All this over seventy years means three generations of Kashmiri people have experienced this directly or indirectly. Getting raped or watching the anguish of your wife or daughter who got raped, which is more? I don't know. I never had to experience either, Alhamdulillah. But I can guess.

Take Manipur. Not one Muslim on the ground. But what's happening there? Same story. Then to top it all we have journalists who write such garbage and papers publish it. Mercifully, the English press has little or no influence in this country. It's what the local language press writes which influences. And I can bet you without seeing a single Kashmiri paper that they are not echoing these sentiments. I have said this before and I will say it to the day I die...The best way to instigate and promote radicalization is to keep attacking Islam. But the world is full of stupid people and their lackeys who will do this to the point where it'll become impossible to control.

There are twenty crore (200 million) Muslims in India. If our extremist anti Muslim elements who'd like to eliminate us, kill one lakh (100,000) every year, it will take them 2000 years to go through the present stock. And while that's happening do you think people will tamely sit by and watch? Force doesn't work in politics. Diplomacy is the key. Until we learn to talk with sincerity, not the baggage loaded parody we see, this will continue and get worse.

The Palestine-Israel conflict is another case in point. Israel tried to use the corrupt PLO to force its illegal occupation. PLO being compromised gave rise to Hamas. Then Hamas got elected legitimately. But Israel and America refuse to recognize a democratically elected party, while they support every despotic dictator in sight using billions of dollars of tax payers money and selling billions of dollars' worth of military equipment thereby making money out of the deaths of innocents. Result??

Israel, with America's backing, unlimited expense account, the best trained, equipped and most ruthless army in the world can't deal with a tiny population inside a walled concentration camp called Gaza. What do you think our leaders will unleash in this country with our demographics by following that policy?

But insanity seems to be a prerequisite of being a politician. The sad thing is that you and I will pay the price.

'We are losing Kashmir to Islam' indeed an excellent article for anyone who wants to rip this country apart.

UCC – Law Commission Questionnaire

An alternate perspective

The ongoing debate on the questionnaire circulated by the Law Commission on the proposed implementation of a Uniform Civil Code and the predictable knee-jerk reaction of the All India Muslim Personal Law Board (AIMPLB) is a very good opportunity to learn the basics of conflict resolution. With over thirty years' experience in negotiation, conflict resolution and arbitration on three continents, working with people of different genders, races, politics, religions and nationalities, I want to share my observations and a perspective of what the course of action could be, an alternative to the boycott of the questionnaire that the AIMPLB has announced.

In negotiation and conflict resolution, one of the most essential skills is to be able to separate the facts from inferences. To separate emotions that those facts or actions may excite. That is not because inference, conjecture and hypothesis are not important. They are. But unless you begin with the basic facts, you will not be able to take objective decisions about them. Only then will the course of action become clear and not one but often more than one alternatives will appear. If one does not begin with facts, then one is only reacting emotionally, which means that one is thinking only in a yes-no way and that is the most difficult and limiting way to think.

It appears to me that the call to boycott the questionnaire is an emotional reaction to the fact that the questionnaire comes from the Law Commission, which is an arm of the government. Given that this government in particular has been responsible for vitiating the peace in the country by remaining silent despite all kinds of violence against Muslims and Dalits in the name of so-called 'Cow Vigilantism', it is only natural that it is not viewed as being Muslim/Dalit friendly. Its agenda to get the UCC implemented and the Muslim Personal Law removed, is well known. But strangely what few have stopped to ask is, 'Why has the government not brought forward the Uniform Civil Code for discussion by all concerned?' The reality is that only that which exists can be implemented. After all the government is not saying, 'We need to create a Uniform Civil Code and then implement it.' It is saying that it wants to implement the UCC. So bring it forward. Let the country see what it is that the government wants to implement.

Laws are not made in the Supreme Court. They are made in the Legislature. So let the UCC be brought before the entire nation. Let the people of India debate it and then let it pass into law in the Legislature. That is the democratic process and let us follow it. What is the need to attempt apparently clandestine moves using the Law Commission? The Law Commission is not the Legislature. Let responsibility be shouldered by those to whom it belongs; the people of India and their elected representatives in Parliament. I am sure nobody can object to following the process.

Having said that, in the famous case of 'Shamim Ara versus state of UP (2002)', the Supreme Court declared triple Talaq invalid and banned. So how can you ban a banned thing? And so therefore why is one of the questions in the Law Commission's questionnaire about triple Talaq? Does the Law Commission seek to do what the AIMPLB didn't do for fourteen years (as of this writing in 2016), i.e. raise the matter of the ban on triple Talaq again? In view of the strident calls to boycott the questionnaire and the claims that the AIMPLB (which interestingly uses the term, 'Muslims of India' unilaterally and without any endorsement from the alleged 'Muslims of India') will not tolerate any 'interference' in the Muslim Personal Law, it is pertinent to ask why this call was not given in 2002? After all the responsibility to fight for our laws didn't suddenly become reality today. So what was the AIMPLB doing for 14 years? Why no protests screaming interference in Personal Law and Shariah?

The questionnaire of the Law Commission is couched in very persuasive language.

http://lawcommissionofindia.nic.in/questionnaire.pdf

I quote from the covering letter of the questionnaire which is titled, 'APPEAL' and which you can read on the link above, "The Law Commission of India welcomes all concerned to engage with us on the comprehensive exercise of the revision and reform of family laws as the Article 44 of the Indian Constitution provides that *'the state shall endeavour to provide for its citizens a uniform civil code throughout the territory of India.' (Italics are mine)*

It is clear from this august beginning that while the Indian Constitution's Article 44 provides that the *'State shall endeavour to provide for its citizens a uniform civil code'*, it didn't specify how this is to be done. There could be several ways to arrive at a uniform civil code ranging from creating a civil code from scratch to borrowing all or parts of it from elsewhere, to using parts of the existing Personal Laws of different religions to arrive at one which is acceptable to everyone. Imagine a Civil Code that takes from everyone to give us all the equivalent of the HUF/Karta/IT concessions, freedom to bear arms, marry four times, and wear turbans and beards (men only please). The grass always looks greener on the other side of the fence. But jokes apart, the questionnaire definitely looks like it is covering some other not-so-noble intentions.

I began with the plea that we need to look at facts. So here are some for us to consider.

Laws don't change social behavior. Let us ask how existing laws have changed the reality for women. If they haven't, and they haven't, then how will new laws do otherwise?

1. Protection of Women from Domestic Violence Act (2005)
2. Indecent Representation of Women (Prohibition) Act (1986)
3. Dowry Prohibition Act (1961)
4. Nirbhaya Act (2013)

The problem is not Talaq, but of men honoring the rights of women. For the record, let me say what I have said many times before; the triple Talaq is not in keeping with the Qur'an and Sunnah. It is not the prescribed way to give Talaq in the Shariah. Triple Talaq is itself a violation of the Shariah and so it is declared Haraam and Bidat by all the

212

jurists and schools of jurisprudence in Islam. How someone can declare something Haraam and Bidat and in the same breath call it valid is something only the brain of a Mufti can understand. Mercifully, I am not blessed with a brain that can think around corners and so I go by what the Book of Allah﷾ says and what His Messengerﷺ did. Neither allowed triple Talaq.

It is strange and indeed laughable that all these emotional declarations by both parties, 'Triple Talaq should be banned' and 'We will not stand for interference in the Shariah', are both apparently ignorant of two cardinal facts:

1. That triple Talaq has already been banned in 2002 (wake up)
2. That its banning has not and will not change the reality of Muslim women at all

However, the difficulties that Muslim women are facing are not a result of Talaq (triple or not) but of the unislamic customs and practices that we have not only allowed into our marriages but have made them mandatory. Islam prohibits dowry. We demand it and it is paid. Islam puts the entire responsibility of incurring all expenses for the marriage on the man, but we insist on dumping them on the woman and she and her family accept this. Islam mandates that marriages must be simple and inexpensive, but we insist on expensive, ostentatious weddings. Islam prohibits any kind of harassment at the time of divorce, if it becomes necessary, but our men do the opposite. All these and more are the real reasons why Muslim women are left high and dry and are the victims of the oppression of their men. How is banning triple Talaq going to solve these problems?

The fact that triple Talaq was banned in 2002, but the problems continue, including the fact that people are still giving triple Talaq, should give the Law Commission (and us) enough cause to pause and reflect if laws alone are enough to bring about social change or whether we have to work together, supporting and helping each other to bring about gender justice. We need to work with sincerity and genuineness and reject all guile, hidden agendas, deception and political jugglery. It is only the truth which will prevail.

So what should the AIMPLB do?

1. Accept that juristic law doesn't have precedence over Divine Writ. Talaq as mentioned in the Qur'an is Divine Writ. Triple Talaq, at best, is juristic law. So declare triple Talaq to be invalid and that it will be counted as one.

2. Declare Halala to be Haraam, which it clearly is. The juristic arguments in its favor are such that I choose not

to mention them here for making those jurists and by inference, Islamic Law, the laughing stock of the world. The AIMPLB knows what those arguments are. They know they are wrong. And so they should declare that Halala is Haraama.

3. Give women a meaningful role in the functioning of the AIMPLB with the power to play a decisive role, especially in matters that concern women. Why should men rule on such matters when we have many highly qualified women scholars and theologians? AIMPLB needs to invite them on the Board and give them positions of authority and real power.

4. Invite prominent Muslim members of civil society (male and female); politicians, academicians, lawyers, businesspeople, journalists, educators, youth leaders, social activists and administrators to become members of the Board. I am happy to provide the Board with an organization structure for this, if they are interested.

5. Move to English as its language of communication because its current language, Urdu, is not the language even all Indian Muslims speak and is a serious impediment in thought share as well as in communicating with the rest of the nation.

6. Set a specific term of office and a retirement age for all Members irrespective of who they may be. Lifetime

employment is detrimental to organizational health and performance.

It is essential that in the world of today and tomorrow the Board evolves to become more representative of all Indian Muslims, if it intends to retain its position as the self-proclaimed leader of Muslims. It must move from being self-proclaimed to acclaimed representative to be truly effective and powerful. To represent, you must be representative. That means more participation, more transparency, more empowerment and more equality. That means that the nature of the Board must change from being an exclusive boys club of elites to becoming a truly democratic, body of equals, all working for the benefit of the nation and the pleasure of our Creator.

For the time will surely come when we will meet Him. And at that time we will not be asked, 'What happened?' We will be asked, 'What did you do?'

What if I Was Asked?

We have been seeing many talk shows and debates on the three questions below, all of which seem to generate more heat than light, providing great TRP ratings for the TV channels airing them and a lot of amusement to viewers. The fact that TV shows don't change laws or the realities on the ground, seems to have escaped all respondents and that combined with the desire to be on TV has led to some very painfully embarrassing reactions.

From my position as a normal, garden variety viewer I have tried to fantasize about how I would answer these questions. Anyone wanting to use these answers is most welcome to do so. You don't even have to quote me.

1. *What is your opinion about the UCC?*

What is your opinion about the Doctrine of Primogeniture? Ha! I can see the surprise on your face. You can't answer me because you don't know what the Doctrine of Primogeniture is. So, let me ask you your own question. What is your opinion about the Uniform Civil Code? I submit to you that you can't answer this question either for the same reason that I can't answer it, which is that neither you nor I know what the UCC is. Therefore, let the Government, if it is serious about its desire to implement the UCC, tell the nation what it is. What is the UCC? Once we, the people of

India, see what the UCC is, then we will be able to tell you our opinion about it.

2. *What do you say about the fact that triple Talaq is oppressive on women?*

I agree. It is oppressive on women in India, thanks to the fact that Indian Muslims have left the Islamic way of marriage and adopted all kinds of customs in their weddings, all of which place a huge financial burden on the wife and her family. The oppression comes from that. Not from the fact that the Talaq is easy to give. The Sunnah way of Talaq is actually easier. The man has to pronounce it only once. Not even thrice. And after the three-month waiting period, the marriage is ended. But I submit to you that the problems of the woman will not be over because all the expense she and her family incurred will still remain. So, what needs to change is the way Muslim marriages are conducted and Muslims need to return to the way that their religion specifies, which is that the bride's family will incur no expense at all and so even if there is a divorce, there will be no material burden on the woman or her family.

What the AIMPLB has decided to do in addition to promoting correct Muslim marriages, is to change our stand with respect to triple Talaq. Triple Talaq in one sitting is not permitted in the Qur'an. Nor was it allowed by Rasoolullahﷺ. So, we have decided to go back to our fundamental and primary sources of law – the Book of Allahﷻ and the Sunnah of His Messengerﷺ and will no longer recognize three Talaqs given in one sitting as three and final. We will follow the way of Rasoolullahﷺ and admonish the man for giving Talaq in such a way and declare that it will amount to only one Talaq with the two extra pronouncements being emphasis and not three individual Talaqs.

3. *What is your response to the questionnaire about the UCC from the Law Commission?*

We thank the Law Commission for its initiative to seek the opinion of the minorities about their Personal Laws. However, we would like to draw the attention of the Law Commission that it is not only the minorities which have Personal Laws. The majority community also has a Personal Law. The questionnaire is a good idea perhaps but it has apparently been drafted in a hurry and so is grossly inadequate.

We would like to help the Law Commission to improve their questionnaire so that it fulfills the needs of all communities in India. So here are two hundred and twenty-three other questions that must be added to the questionnaire. We also suggest that for ease of preserving a record of responses and make it a searchable database for any research or RTI questions which will surely arise and in order to collate and tabulate the response to present them to the Honorable Supreme Court, it is best for the Law Commission to create a website for these questions to be answered. The logistics and expense of that will be far less and easier than a physical paper questionnaire as well as being far more environmental friendly and carbon efficient. These are important factors to consider in such massive nationwide efforts.

Once the new questionnaire is ready it may be sent out, responses collected in due course for which sufficient time must be given, collated and tabulated and presented to the Supreme Court of India. The matter can then be taken forward.

Disclaimer: For those deprived of a sense of humor at birth, please get one. It is free on Amazon. I am NOT a member of the AIMPLB. Never was and never will be. What I have said is my fantasy, not the reality. Never was and who knows if it will ever be. So read on, have a good laugh and go back to sleep.

Urdu – what did I do?

A language, any language, is not simply sounds and script characters which represent thoughts. A language is the soul of the people. It is the vehicle which connects their past to their present, their present to their dreams. It is the means by which one generation leaves its legacy for the next. In my view the single most significant event in human development is the evolution of languages. It was this process that enabled human beings to preserve their thoughts, teach others, learn from history and talk to generations yet unborn. Language is the elixir of eternal life. Or as close to it as we are likely to come.

Among the many strange developments in our country is a resurgence of hostility against Urdu, which is wrongfully alleged to be the language of Muslims. And since Muslims are people non-grata their language is language non-grata. No matter that it has nothing to do with Muslims in the first place. It is seen as that and so it must become unseen. There is a long history to all this and for those who are interested in it, please read this excellent article:

https://thewire.in/226180/a-country-where-sanskrit-deserves-preservation-but-urdu-doesnt/

While I lament the completely undeserved hostility to Urdu, which is in the nature of cutting your nose to spite your face, I must say that nobody and no government can kill a language that people want to use. The very birth and rise of Urdu is testimony to that. Farsi was the official language of the time. Yet Urdu eventually supplanted it without any official support, simply because the people wanted to speak it, wrote in it, transacted business in it and so on. When you read the history of the development of Urdu literature and poetry you can't help being struck by the enormous vitality of the language, its ease of expression, it beauty of turn of phrase, which thanks mainly to the fact that it was understood by the masses, gradually and then rapidly supplanted Farsi. English was repressed in South Africa during the rule of Afrikaners and Afrikaans was strongly propagated to the extent that even today most South African people speak Afrikaans. Yet we know that Afrikaans is dying and will die, and English is alive and well and growing.

The same is true of English in this country which has seen its share of hostility yet all the Hindutva and other chauvinists, send their children to English medium schools for one reason only; because without it they will not have access to the global culture. Languages must cater to the aspirations of people. What happened with Urdu as well as with almost every other Indian language, is that they didn't keep up with scientific development. Indeed, Urdu has some of the most beautiful poetry, especially love poetry in existence. As an Urdu speaker, I can't tell you how it has the power to move me to tears. English poetry on the other hand leaves me cold. There is no other word to describe that. However, when I need to work, think, write my thoughts to an audience that spans borders, it is English that enables me to do so. When I am explaining any concept in science, psychology, sociology or politics, it is English that has the words to describe precisely what I need to say. With Urdu (or Hindi, Tamil, Malayalam and Telugu) I find myself translating the English to create cumbersome and ungainly expressions that make little sense.

Call it my lack of expertise in the Indian languages compared to my mastery of English, the fact remains that this is my experience. Talk to a million others like me and you will find that there are rather a lot of us around. Take that forward and ask how many like me are likely to teach Urdu to our children and you have the perfect diagnosis of the fatal ailment that besets Urdu. I was teaching a leadership course to a group of senior Muslim scholars in Urdu, simultaneously translating my material from English to Urdu when I realized, very painfully, this fact, that Urdu simply doesn't have the words to translate the concepts I was talking about. I did my best and by explaining where I would have used a single word, I managed to do my job, but the fact was clear; Urdu no longer speaks to the modern person. It is like Arabic in a way that has more than twenty words for horse and camel, but not a single one for DNA, corpuscle, neuron or clavicle. Ask yourself, which is more important?

There are many Indian languages which have died over the years, not because someone actively prohibited them, punished those who spoke them and burnt all their literature and poetry, but simply because the people who spoke them, chose not to do so any more. Not a single one of them was spoken by Muslims. Not a single one of them was the target of any Governmental hostility. Yet they all died. Languages die because they no longer have words to express what people want to say. This doesn't happen overnight but is a gradual process, where they fall into disuse. This is what is happening to Urdu. It simply doesn't have the words to cater to our modern world or way of life. The world today has little value for the arts, for sublime thoughts or lofty ideals. It speaks in the language of the present, material, prosaic but real.

Gul o Bulbul kay fasanay hain bahut khoob magar

(Stories of the flower and Bulbul are beautiful but)

Roti tho kamana hi paday ga is mehfil kay baad

(I still have to earn my bread after this gathering)

This is the harsh reality of our life today. No matter how brutal or crass that sounds, language must be utilitarian first. Urdu seems to have lost that race. Incidentally I wrote that couplet just now to illustrate the dilemma of Urdu.

Today Urdu is dying in India, mainly because traditionally Urdu speaking people, Muslims and Hindus, have stopped speaking it. This is the inconvenient truth that those who complain about the impending death of Urdu choose not to face. Ask how many of those who talk of the need to protect Urdu, subscribe to Urdu newspapers? Ask how many children in their homes can read or write Urdu? Ask how many can quote, or even read or memorize Urdu poetry? I am not talking about Islam at all. The language of Islam is Arabic. Not Urdu. I am talking about Urdu literature and poetry; how many can read it, understand it or quote it? The answer is clear and visible before our eyes. But we like to blame the Government when we must look at ourselves first. The fact that Urdu is not the medium of instruction in schools or that it is not an 'official' language, is neither here nor there. Urdu's history is witness that it was not the medium of instruction in schools nor was it the official language yet it supplanted Farsi which was both. It did that without governmental support and despite governmental neglect. It did that for one reason only; because people decided they wanted to use Urdu and not Farsi.

Languages die, not because of the aggression of enemies but the neglect of friends. Aggression may actually help a language which will go underground and remain alive and gain strength thanks to the dangers it faces above ground. This is how Arabic remained alive and well and was taught in secret to Muslim children to enable them to read the Qur'an during the more than eighty years of brutal repression of Islam and all its symbols in erstwhile Soviet Russia. Soviet Russia then became erstwhile. Not Islam or Arabic or the Qur'an.

The situation is not hopeless. Far from it. But the solution doesn't lie in the hands of the Government. It lies in the hands of people. Our hands. The hands of those who claim to love Urdu. Start speaking it yourself. Subscribe to Urdu newspapers. Teach Urdu to your children at home, if schools don't teach it. Listen to Urdu poetry and support Urdu poets. Read Urdu books and write in Urdu. No power on earth can stop you from doing any of this. You don't need any money or time or resources to do any of these. Just the will to get up and do something instead of complaining and blaming the Government. This Government has much it must be held accountable for. But neglect of Urdu is the responsibility of Urdu speaking people. Not the Government.

Yes, the Government of India must support Urdu because it is a truly Indian language. It was born in India, is spoken my millions in India and is a part of the history of India. But before that, Urdu speaking people must support it. If people do it, what the Government does or doesn't do will not matter. If people don't support it, no Government can keep any language alive. Sanskrit is the example to illustrate that. Politicians taking oaths of office in Sanskrit proves nothing. Ask how many speak Sanskrit at home or read Sanskrit papers. Much like Usha Utup singing Hindi songs.

What Comprises Leadership?

What is it that enables some leaders to continue to be inspirational and not lose followers even when their decisions may not be to their follower's liking? This is a very critical dilemma of leadership, of walking the tightrope between populist actions and doing what needs to be done and risk losing popularity. In today's political environment of playing to the gallery, leaders are often held to 'ransom' by their followers who give or withdraw support because they don't like the leader's decision. Or don't understand his wisdom. In modern times, the example of Al Gore comes to mind, where Americans chose George Bush over him for President of America. One can fantasize about how the world would have been different if the author of 'An Inconvenient Truth', had become President. But that is water under the bridge.

So, what is it that sets a leader apart where even when he proposes to do what his followers either don't understand or don't like, they still support him and commit to his way and he doesn't lose trust in their eyes?

The two finest examples of this in Islamic history are the Treaty of Hudaybiyya and the Wars of Riddah. Let us see the challenges that the leaders faced in each of them.

Suleh Hudaybiyya

I won't narrate the history of this very famous treaty as it is well known. I will list the challenges that Rasoolullahﷺ faced. They were perhaps the most severe challenges that any leader could have faced, especially one who was the Messenger of Allahﷺ and so the recipient of Wahi (Revelation). He took the people with him on Umrah, naturally with the intention of performing Umrah but thanks to a series of events which obviously he could not have anticipated, he was now in the process of signing a treaty that was so one-sided as to be humiliating for the Muslims. Two of the most difficult to accept clauses were:

1. They must return to Madina without making Umrah
2. If a Muslim left Islam and went over to the Quraysh of Makkah he/she would be given refuge and need not be returned to Madina. But if a non-Muslim accepted Islam and went from Makkah to Madina, he/she must be returned to Makkah and must not be given refuge.

To add to the difficulty, Abu Jandal *bin* Suhayl﷜ the brother of Abdullah *ibn* Suhayl﷜ and *son* of Suhayl *Ibn Amr*, the orator of Quraysh had accepted Islam and consequently had been imprisoned by his father, escaped and came to Hudaybiyya having heard that Rasoolullahﷺ was camped there. His father Suahyl ibn Amr was the representative of Quraysh, negotiating the treaty. The clauses of the treaty had been agreed upon but had not been written down yet. He demanded that his son should be handed over to him to be returned to Makkah in chains and Rasoolullahﷺ agreed. He advised Abu Jandal﷛ to be patient when he complained that the Quraysh would punish him for accepting Islam. The Sahaba were horrified because what was happening was directly against the custom of giving refuge to a victim and in this case to a fellow Muslim. Yet Rasoolullahﷺ was honoring the clause of a treaty even though it had not yet been signed. He was honoring his word which had been given, the writing of which was merely detail. The Sahaba were very sad and angry.

Sad about not being able to enter Makkah and make Umrah and angry at what the Quraysh were demanding. Omar ibn Al Khattab﷛ even went the extent of questioning Rasoolullahﷺ. Once again, I will not go into the details here as these are well known. However, I would like to say that his questioning was really the unconscious expression of the doubt in the minds of many others, if not most. It was a cry of anguish in the face of the apparently placid and submissive acceptance of injustice. Yet when all was said and done, the Sahaba stood behind Rasoolullahﷺ solidly and followed him and did as he instructed them to do. And that is the bottom-line and the question that I raise here,

'What was it about Rasoolullahﷺ that inspired them to follow him, even when his decision was not to their liking?'

To better understand the challenge from the perspective of the followers (Sahaba) let me list some of the obvious doubts that this entire incident raises. I am not saying that the Sahaba had these doubts. Allahﷻ knows what was in their minds and hearts and that is not the subject of our discussion here. This is an objective analysis of one of the most severe tests of leadership in history which is important for us to understand. I call this the 'final exam', which qualified the Sahaba in the sight of Allahﷻ to lead the world and Heﷻ opened for them not only the doors of Makkah but the whole of their world. Hudaybiyya was the toughest exam because it was not a test of bravery or physical prowess, but a test of faith and trust. The Sahaba passed it with flying colors.

The doubts that the incident raises are:

1. They believed in Muhammadﷺ as the Messenger of Allahﷻ who received Revelation (Wahi). They believed that one of the forms in which Wahi was received was in a dream. Rasoolullahﷺ had seen in his dream that he was making Umrah with his companions and so, had invited them to join him to travel to Makkah to make Umrah. However, now he was agreeing not to make

Umrah that year and was going to return to Madina with them without fulfilling the intention of performing Umrah.

2. They had been taught and believed that Islam was the truth. They had been taught and believed that standing up for the truth and fighting against falsehood was a sacred trust and duty. Yet here they were apparently giving in to blatant injustice.

3. They now faced the prospect of returning to Madina to the taunts of the Munafiqeen who would no doubt cast aspersions on the prophethood and veracity of Rasoolullah ﷺ.

4. For Rasoolullah ﷺ himself were the questions, 'If Allah ﷻ wanted him to make Umrah, why did this barrier come about? Why did Allah ﷻ not open the door for him to make Umrah after directing him to do so in his dream? Why was Allah ﷻ wanting him to sign such a humiliating treaty with his enemies? What 'face' would he have with his followers who believed in his Messengership? What about his personal credibility as the Messenger of Allah ﷻ?'

Truly Hudaybiyya was a test, difficult beyond belief. That is why I call it the 'final' exam of the Sahaba.

Wars of Riddah

Before we discuss the reasons for the Sahaba remaining steadfast in their support for Rasoolullahﷺ let me mention another similar incident in early Muslim history which was a landmark for the future of Islam. This was the refusal of many tribes to pay Zakat, after the death of Rasoolullahﷺ. They refused on the grounds that they used to pay it to Rasoolullahﷺ who was no longer present and so Zakat was not due any longer. Abu Bakr Siddique﷑ the Khalifa reminded them that Zakat was not a personal payment to Rasoolullahﷺ but was a Rukn (Pillar) of Islam about which Rasoolullahﷺ had declared that anyone who separated Salah from Zakat had left Islam. It was on this basis that Rasoolullahﷺ had refused to accept the Islam of the Banu Thaqeef of At-Ta'aif when they came to him and offered to accept Islam on condition that they be made exempt from paying Zakat. Rasoolullahﷺ refused and declared that both Salah and Zakat were Pillars of Islam and equal in importance and that leaving of either would be tantamount to leaving Islam. On this basis, Abu Bakr Siddique﷑ declared war on those tribes who refused to pay Zakat.

The Sahaba were very perturbed about this as it appeared that the Khalifa Abu Bakr Siddique﷑ was planning to make war on Muslims. Omar ibn Al Khattab﷑ asked Abu Bakr﷑ how he could consider going to war against Muslims. Abu Bakr﷑ said to him, 'What has happened to you Omar, that you were very tough when you were not a Muslim but have become soft after entering Islam?' He then reminded him about the ruling of Rasoolullahﷺ about separating Zakat from the rest of Islam and said, 'Even if they refuse to give a single rope of a camel which is due, I will fight them.' And that is what he did. In retrospect, it was this single unshakable stance of Abu Bakr Siddique﷑ which preserved the integrity of Islam after Rasoolullahﷺ passed away. If he had not taken this firm stand, Islam would perhaps have disintegrated with people deciding to follow whatever suited them. But ask, 'What is it that made the Sahaba support him even when they disagreed with his decision?'

In the case of Rasoolullahﷺ at Hudaybiyya, one could say that his position as being the Messenger of Allah﷽ was sacrosanct and when you believed that he was receiving Revelation, it was perhaps easier to follow without question. However, Abu Bakr﷑ was not receiving Revelation. He was one among them, albeit first among equals, but an equal. Yet they obeyed him even though some or many didn't agree with his decision, initially. Not only did they obey him, but they put their own lives on the line and enrolled in the conscript army which was the army of the time. Nobody stayed back. Nobody said, 'I don't agree and so I am not going to risk my life by joining the army.' What made them do that?

I believe there were two major characteristics that operated in both these incidents; i.e. Hudaybiyya and the Wars of Riddah.

1. **Trustworthiness:** An unshakable faith beyond question in the personal credibility of the leader. This faith was based on the character of the leader which his followers had seen throughout his life and which inspired total trust and respect in their hearts. So, while they may have disagreed with the leader in a matter, his personal credibility, his intention that he wished the best for them, his objectivity, truthfulness, commitment to the goal (Islam), impartiality, lack of selfishness, sincerity, desire only to please Allah﷾ were never in question.

2. **Respect:** The belief that the leader was more knowledgeable, committed and sincere than any one of them. That he understands a situation better than the follower. That his track record shows that even in the past he had been right, when he differed with his followers.

As you can see, these two factors are dynamically linked. One supports the other. And both arise out of one's conduct. When you live by your principles, you don't have to keep talking about them. People see them in your life and emulate them in their own. The converse is equally true which we tragically see in our modern-day leadership. Leaders who don't walk their talk may be obeyed out of fear but are never respected and loved. There is no way that a leader can divorce his personal conduct from his stated principles and expect followers to respect and follow his lead.

Personal credibility which translates to high respect. People trust those they respect. And they don't trust those who lose respect in their estimation. A leader's life is public. Every statement, whether made in seriousness or jest, is public. Every action, private or public, personal or involving others, is public. And they all contribute to the overall picture of the leader that people hold in their minds. Image and personal credibility of the leader is built on his walking the talk. People listen with their eyes and don't care what you say until they see what you do. This is the Brand of the leader. They care less about what is being said, than about who is saying it. 'How' also matters, but only after 'Who'. If people don't respect the individual, what he/she says doesn't matter.

First the who, then the how and then the what. Seems strange but that is human psychology for you. People must first trust a leader. Then they listen to how he puts across his proposal. Then they think about what he is asking them to do. If the first two, especially the first one (high personal credibility), is strong, people will even go to extraordinary lengths to follow their leaders.

In times of stress, success of the leader depends on the ability of followers to recall and remember the brand. And still obey and follow the leader and commit themselves even when they don't fully understand why they should commit. And even when they may not agree with some of what the leader is doing. Please note that what I am referring to is not what happens after the leader has explained what he is doing and why he wants their support. I am talking about a time when the leader may not have the time, opportunity or may for reasons of confidentiality, decide on a course of action without consulting his team. Will the team still follow him and commit fully to him and his course or will they hold back, rebel and not support? That is the meaning of faith in the leadership. Like all good things, maybe easier said than done, but like flying, if you want to fly, you must be aerodynamic. There is no alternative.

Who are the friends of Fake News?

I expect most of you, if not all, saw this post on WhatsApp about how and why fake news spreads faster than real news. For those who didn't here it is.

http://money.cnn.com/2018/03/08/media/fake-news-mit-study/index.html

This is a ten plus year MIT study which comes up with many surprising findings one of which is: *"A surprising twist in the study was that bots spread fake news at the same rate as true news, suggesting, "False news spreads more than the truth because humans, not robots, are more likely to spread it."*

What does fake news do?

It results in violence, hatred, death, destruction of property and disruption of lives. Perhaps one day, your own. Self-interest seems to be the only effective deterrent today in a world that seems to be free of any sense of community, responsibility, compassion or accountability. So be it. Think of yourself at the end of the fake news, if that is what it takes to prevent you from spreading fake news. All it takes is one click. All it takes to do the opposite is not to do that one click.

What must you do when you receive stuff that people ask you to forward?

1. Simply use your head. Look at the fake news below, which I am sure you have all seen; the so-called anti-corruption drive with a list of names of all those who allegedly have money hidden in Swiss banks.

- WIKI LEAKS Published 1st List of black money holders in SWISS bank...... The Top Most 30 members are.....(money is in CRORES)
- 1 - Ambani (568000)
- 2 – Adani (7800)
- 3 - Amit Shah (158000)
- 4 - Rajnath Singh (82000)
- 5 - Arun Jaitley (15040)
- 6 - Smriti Irani (28900)
- 7 - Yadiyurappa (9000)
- 8 - Ravi Shankar Guruji (15000)
- 9 - Baba Ramdev (75000)
- 10 - Janard Jana Reddy (50000)
- 11 - Nalin Kohli (5900)
- 12 - Devendra Fadnavis (220000)
- 13 - Lalit Modi (76888)
- 14 - Sushma Swaraj (582114)
- 15 - Narendra Modi (19800)
- 16 - Harshad Mehta (135800)
- 17 - Ketan Parekh (8200)
- 18 - Katta Subramanya Naidu (14500)
- 19 - Lalu Prasad Yadav (28900)
- 20 - J M Scindia (9000)
- 21 - Kalanidi Maran (15000)
- 22 - Vaiyapuri Gopalaswamy (35000)
- 23 - Vasundhara Raje (5900)
- 24 - Raj foundation (189008
- 25 - N Chandrbabu (168009)
- 26 - J.Jayalalitha (257500)
- 27 - Soniya Gandhi (300089)
- 28 - Subramaniya swamy (220060)
- 29 - Sasi Kala (154700)
- 30 - T.T.V.Thenakaran (12870)
- pls fwd this msg by post on your wall.....pls support the movement against Corruption
- Undigestible news: Indians black money in Swiss bank is Rs. 358,679,863,300,000 (estimated to be 1.3 trillion dollars) this money belongs to 2000 Indians who have kept there to evade from tax, This money is enough for our India to become 10 america and become one of the most powerful developed country in the world for next 100yrs..Please raise your hand by forwarding this to all if you have free messages..As an INDIAN I am Forwarding...

Then read the passionate appeal at the end and ask if the person writing this can do simple math. The US, at last count, was a \$13 trillion economy. How then can \$1.3 trillion, if brought back from Swiss banks, make India ten times bigger than the US? So, the real question is not whether the one who posted this nonsense knows math but whether, you, Mr/Mrs/Ms Forwarder, do?

Take another one about the construction of a mosque in a football stadium. Sounds like a nice cosy, cuddly story of love and mutual respect and would have been if it were true. Here is the story:

> - Here's the intro fyi ☟(Bayern Munich is one of the leading football in Germany)"Bayern Munich, the club's official website, announced the opening of a mosque at the Allianz Arena, a stronghold of the Bavarian club, and it will be the first mosque in any world stadium.The initiative came after Frenchman Bilal Ribery (Frank Ribery) a striker with the club, proposed to the club management that they allocate a small room for prayer on the pitch for him and other Muslim players.But the reaction of the management of the club was unexpected, as they ordered the building of a proper mosque for Muslim players and fans and with an imam and his office together with Islamic and science workshops and paid 85% of the value of construction and the rest made up by the players and fans who wanted to contribute to the construction of the mosque and obtain the rewards. This is the mosque. Watch the shoe compartments where they are equipped with lights to indicate vacant (green) and occupied (red).Not just does this exhibit true Islamic values amongst the people but the creativity of the Germans in the mosque set up is truly very Islamic as well. Unbelievable. A mosque of this architecture at Alianz Arena in Germany!☟☟

And here is my simple investigation:

The mosque mentioned is a Turkish mosque in Germany and not in the Allianz area. This is the mosque: https://www.youtube.com/watch?v=6oIichi5CuU

No mention of any mosque on the official website of the club. See for yourself.

https://allianz-arena.com/en/search

2. Verify the fake news. It is quite easy. Go to https://www.snopes.com/ and type in your fake news or read their archives and you will discover whether it is

true or false. Microsoft is not giving away free computers, Ericsson is not giving away free phones and NASA didn't announce that the sun has risen in the West. To verify videos please go to https://www.snopes.com/video/

3. Mindless fans of Justin Beiber are called 'Beliebers'. Really. Mindless forwarders of fake news, what shall we call them? 'Believers': those who believe without thinking.

   https://www.urbandictionary.com/define.php?term=Belieber

4. And finally, the easiest thing to do; **DO NOTHING**. Hit 'Delete'. And use the baseball rules: 3 strikes is OUT. In this case, anyone who sends you fake news thrice, block him, ban him and delete him from your address book.

5. For those who still want to continue to forward fake news imagining that writing, 'AS RECEIVED' saves you, please wake up and stop smoking whatever keeps you in your haze of fantasy; it doesn't. Not in this life or the next. In this life, forwarding fake stuff can land you in jail. In the next life you will be called to account for having forwarded stuff that led to all kinds of pain and suffering for others. You read it, you decided to forward it, so you are RESPONSIBLE. It is as simple as that.

www.ingramcontent.com/pod-product-compliance
Lightning Source LLC
Chambersburg PA
CBHW072256260726
48658CB00001BA/86